Endorsements for *Excitable Boy*

In these essays, Gordon pokes the bruise that society leaves on those who push back. Shining a light on characters who reliably fall between the cracks, he dares you to flinch.

Jenny Valentish

Nightclub fights, graffiti odysseys. The lube-stink of low rent sex clubs, lust for life told with humour and style. Great, great writing. An instant classic.

Guy Rundle

The experience of reading Dominic Gordon's powerful journey in Melbourne at the turn of the century reminded me of first encountering Jim Carroll's *The Basketball Diaries*.

Brin-Jonathan Butler, podcast host

Excitable Boy

Dominic Gordon

Dominic Gordon is from Melbourne. His work has appeared *Meanjin, The Suburban Review, Visible Ink* and other literary journals. In 2016 he created and produced a radio play that was broadcast on Radio National's, Soundproof program, called Cooked in the Big Smoke. In 2018 Dominic was awarded a Berry Street Fellowship at the State Library of Victoria. Excitable Boy: Essays on Risk is his first book.

Dominic Gordon

Excitable Boy

Essays on risk

First published in Australia in 2024
by Upswell Publishing
Perth, Western Australia
upswellpublishing.com

Upswell operates in the city of Perth, on ancient country of the Whadjuk people of the Noongar nation who remain the spiritual and cultural custodians of this beautiful land. We acknowledge their continuing connection to country and express gratitude to elders past and present for their strength and creativity...Always was, always will be, Aboriginal land.

ISBN: 978-0-645-87455-6

A catalogue record for this book is available from the National Library of Australia

Author note: many names have been changed in this book but nothing else, because it all happened.

Cover design by Chil3, Fremantle
Typeset in Foundry Origin by Lasertype
Printed by McPherson's Printing Group

For Roie. And our beautiful son Elmore.

And to the lost boys who went wandering
and never made it home, this is for you.

Contents

After ten long years they let him out of the home
Excitable Boy, they all said
And he dug up her grave and built a cage with her bones
Excitable Boy, they all said
Well, he's just an Excitable Boy

Warren Zevon

Introduction

Christos Tsiolkas

Nearly ten years ago now, Dominic Gordon approached me and asked – tentatively, diffidently – if I might be interested in reading a manuscript he was working on. I said yes, because I trusted my gut instinct: this was someone who was serious about writing. He didn't speak in cliches, and he didn't pretend a false humility. He spoke of writing – and of movies and of life – with a clear purpose and ardour.

I was impressed with the voice that emanated from the pages he gave me. The language was raw, rough, but there was a no-bullshit vividness in his writing that I responded to immediately. The other thing that I remember distinctly about that first encounter with his work, was how unsettling it was to read him. There was something almost frightening in the clarity and unsentimentally of his storytelling. There was nothing safe and polite in his words. To be honest, there wasn't much I could offer him except to urge him to keep writing, and to keep reading – and maybe I added, 'Avoid the pitfalls of fashion.'

We're not friends, we've seen each other a handful of times since 2014. Yet there would be moments over the next decade when I was walking my city, Melbourne, and his voice would return to me. His writing was a map of the city that I had never encountered before in any other writer's work. It was subterranean and dark and dirty and strange and thrilling and dangerous. There was nothing academic in his writing. There was precise and evocative detail in his stories and essays, but they weren't journalistic. I recall my friend and mentor,

Sasha Soldatow, saying to me once that there were 'born writers'. Meaning that there is a talent, a gift for language, that springs off the page even when the craft is still being developed, when the technical skills are still to be learnt. I think Dominic Gordon is a born writer.

When I received the manuscript for *Excitable Boy*, I was nervous. Would his talent have been tamed? I shouldn't have doubted him. His writing still unsettles. This book is a journey through space and through time, about a city and about a body, and the prose is hard, and the prose is sensual. You smell the city and the body. It is also a book about lives lived in the underworld that doesn't have a hint of self-pity or sanctimony. Gordon's writing is more assured now, and the risk-taking is more confident, and so that makes the toughness of his prose more compelling.

I think of this book as notes from the underground written from the other side of gentrification. Not from the clean and bourgie and university side of that divide, but from the *other* side, the one that rarely makes it into our published writing. Not that Gordon's writing is vain or smug. It is so *not* worthy. It is harsh and it is vitally alive, and it is quietly tragic. But that's what life is, on *that* side.

I finished *Excitable Boy* in a rush, and when I finally exhaled, I recalled Rosa Cappielo's *Oh Lucky Country*, another Australian book that speaks in a voice that I had never heard before. It's rare when that happens, and it is astonishing: a writer punching you in the gut, making you recognise that you don't know as much as you think you know. It is how I felt after reading Fiona McGregor's *Chemical Palace* and Eric Michael's *Unbecoming*. All these books share that wondrous daring to travel unflinchingly to places where most of us are too timid or too scared to go. I love those books precisely because they don't play it safe. And it is why I love *Excitable Boy*.

Dominic Gordon takes writing seriously. I knew that from our first meeting. This book is a journey through the night and a journey through the underground. He's an unsettling guide, but you can absolutely trust him.

1
The Adelphi Hotel

The Adelphi is a five-star, boutique, chrome, minimalist hotel in the heart of the CBD. It has a salt-water pool on the roof. You can see a slice of the rich blue water, David Hockney painting, brown skin lounging, urban paradise jutting out from the street. I've snuck into many hotel pools in the CBD, but never the Adelphi. It's the jewel in the crown.

It looks a bit complicated to get in, so I stand across the street from it and just watch for a while as people flow past me. No-one takes notice of me. I'm small and quick and avoid eye contact. The reception is just inside. I see some guy about to go in. I run over and cruise in behind. I pretend I'm with him. He's wearing bright pink pants with a canary-yellow jumper draped over his shoulders. His solarium-browned, sizzled English criminal-in-Majorca head is offset by a crisp white shirt. We go in the lift. Solarium Steve slides off on the fifth floor. I need to go to the top. The doors ding open on six and I see the stairwell. I go up the stairs and see the sign that says 'swimming pool'. I open it.

It's just like I imagined. I'll pool the rich scumbags' resources any time. The gold brochure liquefies and fills me to the brim with false pride. Just a little bit. Just a taste, that's all I want. A gently sloshing credit-card-slim pool up against the edge, five red-and-white-striped deck chairs, artificial grass and a strip of hot concrete with complimentary slippers all over it. It's like a film crew has broken for lunch. I crouch down and dip my hand in the water. I take off everything except my jocks and bomb in. I close my eyes and float, limbs outstretched in a womb-like stillness. I'm in the middle of the ocean. Schools of fish cruise by in a ball then zip away. I can't remember the last time I was this calm. I gotta hold my breath more often. A shadow shimmies across the ocean. I jump up and deep breathe.

He's standing over the pool concentrating calmly on the water. He is long and sharp and resembles a comfortable insect. He wears a wolf-grey Ralph Lauren tracksuit with a white insignia. The tracksuit rounds off his sharpness. He also wears black sunglasses and rocks the hotel slippers. He gracefully removes a slipper and dips in a white toe that's basically translucent. He speaks in my general direction.

'The water is nice.'

The water ripples from his toe, and when the ripples hit my chest, I wince. He puts his toe back in the slipper and glides over to a deck chair. I respond cautiously.

'Yes, it's nice.'

He removes his tracksuit. He's wearing navy-blue speedos that look like they're made of velvet. His scrawny white body looks like it should be in a hospital. He has marks all over him and dodgy tattoos. The insect lowers his glasses. He has goggly black eyes. Tone flat like the Autobahn.

'I haven't seen you here before.'

There's a tight smile behind the glare.

'I came in with the canary.'

He leans back, gets out a cigarette and lights it, smiling.

'You have to watch that canary. He sings a little too loud.'

I want to laugh but I feel that if I do, I'll somehow be in his debt. I duck under the water and frog-leg a while. When I resurface, I come face to face with him. He's on his haunches. He has taken off his sunglasses.

'Fancy a martini, kid?'

I feel like he has the secrets to the things I never knew I wanted to know. They are written around the lines in his pupils.

'Sure.'

The sun has been swallowed by clouds. I get out of the pool. I have no towel. I stand there dripping. I can feel each drop of water run off my body and splash on the concrete in slow motion. The insect gets on the poolside phone and orders some drinks. I lie down on a deck chair. He turns to me.

'Chuck this towel over you when they bring the drinks.'

I do as he says. I rarely do as anyone says. A waitress brings out two drinks on a silver tray. She puts them down and leaves. We sip and stay silent in the shade of the large beach umbrellas. The pool sloshes around and the surrounding buildings prison us in. Hard city shapes chop and change, jabbing in and out of each other like unfinished conversations. I converse with concrete geometry and we agree on some matters. My eyes drift from the outlines of the city and back to the sun-splashed pool. The salt water has coated me in its peace. I look at my salty white body with the wiry hairs on my chest and feel the salt coat. I suddenly do not like this situation. I refuse to wear anyone else's coat. Salty fabric body crust, I will not fucking adjust! I jump off the sun lounge and spill my drink all over the artificial grass.

'Fuck this coat.'

The insect lowers the shades.

'What's wrong, kid?'

'Who the fuck are you, with your what's wrong? You don't know me.'

I'm up in his face now.

'Chill out, kid.'

'I'm not your kid, kid.'

He laughs and slurps some drink.

'Come on then, I'll show you something.'

He gets up, slips on his slippers and glides away. I stand there staring at him. The buildings behind me breathe down my neck.

His room is spotless. He goes over to the bed. I stop at the door. I watch him real close. He takes out a fifty-cent coin and bounces it on top of the blanket. It bounces twice. He seems satisfied.

'Gotta have a tight ship for a crisp sleep, right kiddo?'

I also like a well-made bed, but I don't bounce coins. He gestures for me to sit. I do. He sits in a wicker chair by the window. The curtains dance around in the hot wind casting shadows over his face. He eye-balls me.

'I saw you lift that wallet at Flinders Street. It was nice work.'

The dodgy insect must be an old hand. That's the connection. The way he moves. His style. His command of the moment. I was unknowingly respecting his presence. I still have the wallet wrapped up in my T-shirt. His black eyes are no longer as threatening. He kicks his head back and winks. I also kick my head back. I put the T-shirt down. My pipe is in my shoe. The two points are in my sock. Contraband heavy. But I get the feeling he doesn't care. I relax my limbs and ask.

'How long you been living in this room?'

He looks around at the immaculate interior. The only thing on his wall is an A3-sized black-and-white framed photo of the Flinders Street steps from 1986.

'Ten years.'

His words drift into the air and I see them vanish out the window. He carries himself like an elegant chief of a forgotten tribe. His face is deep and wrinkled. The years have scarred him well. If he ever cried, tears would run down his map in multiple rivulets. He drops in and out of focus as though my lens is up against a constantly moving object. I look around his room. Imagine living in a hotel for ten years. I mean, it's a pretty nice room, but ten years in any one place is a long time. I think about one of my favourite books as a child: *Eloise*. An illustrated book about a girl who lived in the Plaza Hotel in New York. She ran amok. Had a great time. I wanted to do that when I was that age, but now, I dunno.

'Don't you ever want to leave this place?'

He shrugs his sharp shoulders and looks over my head.

'Maybe I'll leave one day. I'll just have to wait and see.'

We sit in silence. He lights a ciggy, smiles and gazes around like a calm insect sitting on a giant blade of grass. I cannot sit in silence for too long. Already it's too long. I crunch the air.

'Do you mind if I have a toke?'

The blade-of-grass vibe changes.

'It's your soul, kid.'

Damn right it is. I've got a big soul. Bigger than the pipe. What does he know about my soul?

'You never tried it?'

He has some kind of electric spasm and explodes.

'Why do you think I live in this fucking hotel!'

Cracks harden then instantly become slack. An animal of extreme power. His aggression engages me. Deadpan:

'Cos you like the pool?'

He chuckles.

'Yeah, cos I like the pool.'

I slide the pipe out from my sock, shimmy it into my palm. Dirty inescapable pipe. I'm gonna smoke. It is my soul. I see the dark. I see the light. I see the insect move and it looks like he's getting into storytelling mode. I recognise the transition of body structure. It used to happen to my dad when he was about to reveal. The posture, inquisitive and hunched over, leaning in with his elbows on his knees, is identical. Then he stands up, looks out the window and down onto the street. He sits down again and stares at me. I'm about to prepare the pipe, but it's full of old gunk from epic tokes and needs a clean. I point at the bowl.

'Mind if I clean it?'

He points at an oven mitt on the stove. I go to the stove and shove my left hand in the mitt. I turn on a burner on the stove and, with mitted hand, put the glass over the direct blue heat. The shimmering, glassy blue orange heat. Soon, it's clean. I let it cool then pack it up. The show is about to begin. The insect smiles.

'It was 1998. I was 16. Everyone was getting cooked.'

He's up and about like he's just come on the ground. I'm twirling deep clouds now, channeling ballerina masculinity with a dip of the wrist.

'Then it appeared on the scene. Nobody knew what it was. Just some stronger whippa. That's all.'

Smoke fills the room and he's cutting in and out of memory mist. I'm watching a movie. The main character is me. It is Melbourne. It is my choice to be an actor in this world. Active. Not passive. Aggressive. I'm the screenwriter. I'm the director. Who is the editor? Godly fucking editor.

'Then it was only ice, and it was everywhere. Pure as fuck. We also used to rort a bit but just for fun. Soon, we had no money.'

I plume the insect shrouding his raw deal. The story of then has fused with now. Cross-pollination across a generational divide. He's sliding right back with his words. I'm struggling a bit at the fact that I have become the bad influence on the older insect. But just toke and it becomes a joke. Pain shimmying away like a spineless creature in a stagnant pond.

'We had to get cash. Nobody wanted to work. Soon there was me and two mates creepin around doing day-time burgs and picking pockets. We were good. But nobody is that good. We got pinched and pinched again. I went to jail. I was twenty-one. That was that.'

I ask him – as I put the pipe to rest on a coin on the bedside table – about how he ended up in the hotel.

'I met some guys in jail that had even lighter fingers than me. When I got out, I got busy again. One night I had nowhere to stay and a fair bit of coin, so I booked a room at the Adelphi and bunkered down.'

'I'd already smoked enough to keep me awake for three days, but I had nothing else to do.'

He glides over to the pipe. I ask his eyes:

'How long since…'

He's big enough to look after himself, right? I am the one who needs looking after. Not the insect. He stares deep into me.

'I panicked that night. I called the ambulance. I cried to a plump paramedic called Judy, I was dying. Judy reassured me I wasn't. They monitored me and left. I tried to leave the city. But I couldn't. Every time I tried to leave, I would get violently ill and run back to my hotel room. Back into the city. Since then, I've never left.'

It begins to rain. We look towards the window. The sun is still out. I can't be sure if it's actually raining or whether the insect's stash of un-cried tears have finally been set free and all this is happening inside his head. I am living this moment from within his perspective. The Adelphi is a room in a section of memory bank that we are both invested in. It's cold swimming in spinal fluid.

'Ten years since I smoked, kid.'

It would feel too strange to give advice to someone so much older than me about what not to do. I can't bring myself to do it. He leans in, pops the goggles and nods.

'Pack it up, kid.'

I do it for him. I do it for me. I do it for the trajectory of our moment. It is a special occasion, and this is how I celebrate. I drop in a point and pass it to his trembling hands. The insect becomes a vacuum cleaner on the highest setting. After a bit, he switches off the vac.

'Kid, this is prime-time filth. Where's it from?'

'Out west.'

The twinkle in the eye. Hardcore substance without genuine substance forced sustenance for something greater. Is it my fault, his, whose? Lock it down with no answers. He gets mildly serious, gets up off his throne and gestures for me to do the same. The insect cruises around on a low cloud. He's shed the outer layer of his tracksuit. He wears a white T-shirt and tracksuit pants. Long thin arms bopping by his side. Words on his skin. Inside the crook of his left elbow is the word 'dip'. An arrangement of beautiful derangement. He nods at me through a million years. It was inevitable our street moves would melt into our natural rhythm. He glides over to a stereo and puts on some music.

'You like Kid Creole and the Coconuts?'

'Tropical Gangsters?

'Nice.'

The track 'Stool Pigeon' slips out, drowning in the fat dopamine stream. Motherfucker, the insect can really move. He's prancing about, limbs on the bend, knees liquid. He stops mid-lurch. The praying mantis on pause. He's frowning.

'"Stool Pigeon." Shit, I never checked to see if you're wearing a wire, kid.'

His eyes goggle dangerously. I'm small next to him. I laugh it off.

'Are you fucken kidding?'

He comes closer so all I can see are black holes in a slippery mask.

'I never thought to check. I finally had someone who could listen to me, but you've probably been wearing a wire all along. "Stool Pigeon" is your song.'

He laughs.

'Haha, had ya there, kid.'

Fuckin nutcase. Fuckin nutcase in the Adelphi nutcase. Street preacher teacher nutcase. Keep him away from the ice fuckin nutcase. Who knows how long we've been cutting it up? All I know is that it is now dark. The room is dark. Everything is dark. I squint in the new dark over at him. He's sweating profusely in a cloak of skin. The human insect in the rainforest sitting on his chiefly throne dripping away his life. I check my phone. It's 10 pm. I grab the pipe and put it in the sock. I gather up my things. I need to go. His words drift across slow from the throne.

'You leaving kid?

'Yep, gotta be somewhere out there. This room is frying the scone.'

His face shifts in and out of the shadows.

'Do you have to leave, kid?'

Is that real sadness?

'Can you stay?'

'Ahh, I'm getting cabin fever man. I gotta hit the air. You all right?'

The insect is starting to droop on his throne. He's actually sliding downwards. He speaks from the slide.

'You're gonna just take off?'

This is too much.

'I can't breathe in here any more, man. I have trouble breathing. I have asthma ya know.'

I get out my puffer from my back pocket. I inhale some Ventolin into my lungs in a fake move that instantaneously becomes real once I start acting. There's no sound from the throne. Then I hear sobbing. Quiet, deep sobbing. I go over to him. He looks drained of life, folding in on himself like a broken family folding chair. I crouch down in front of him.

'You'll be all right man. You'll see. You've lasted this long. The show will go on.'

He can't stop crying. I want to cry too, face to face with the insect. He has been a momentary mentor to me but now I have to be the mentor to him. I am not equipped. I close my eyes and squint real hard till it hurts but I can't manufacture a single fucking tear. He screams at me with wide eyes bubbling spittle anger.

'You dirty thief. You dirty fucking thief!'

I wipe the spit off my face. I get up. I back away. His eyes are wild and chromium black like oil has spilt in his brain. I tell him:

'I'm sorry. I won't forget you.'

He starts to fade from view in the alien light. I grab the door handle and almost rip it off its hinges. I look back and see my mentor turn into a puddle on the chair and drip down to the floor in soundless drops. I'm trembling all over when I smash the air. I look up to where the insect's room was. There is no light on. A bit further up on the roof, the black water sloshes around gently. I take off down Flinders Lane.

2
State Library Victoria

It's mid-2017, a year or so before the State Library Victoria had its massive philanthropic facelift, before the dozens of free access computers either side of a boulevard-esque walkway were removed to be replaced with a giant empty space, renamed The Quad. Its defining feature being how little it resembled anything to do with a library. Two other spaces were added, Ideas Quarter and Create Quarter. Mostly empty. At least they kept the 10 am opening time. I'm here now at 10:03, walking up the boulevard on the way to the Redmond Barry Reading Room with my black backpack. In it: books, a laptop, a banana. Straps pulled tight, measured out like shoelaces. If I'm not at the State Library, sometimes I'll go to City Library. North Melbourne Library occasionally. I even took a holiday on the tram down to Docklands Library, which is basically a sleek hardwood Nordic living room with harbour views, far too distracting to get anything done.

Today, the boulevard is busy. I pass the pensioner with the God beard who carries a Vegemite jar concealed in a jacket pocket of his pea coat. A portable spittoon. To his credit, he buries his head in his coat to spit, before closing the lid, securing the jar. A few computers across, an old woman with wild pink hair and shopping bags full of documents is squinting at a block of text, tapping away with both index fingers. She reminds me of a resident who lived in a halfway house in Richmond where I shared a small room with a friend for a while, at a strange time in my life, a few years ago. I keep moving and am almost at the end of the boulevard when I look over at a computer as a boxing match on

YouTube catches my eye. Being a boxing nerd, I slow down. It's Ali vs Foreman, Rumble in the Jungle. And sitting at the computer is a middle-aged man with a silver buzzcut, who, from that moment on, started popping up everywhere. It turned out that he was also a State Library tragic, and would sit in the same place every time, a stone's throw from where I sat.

I'm not sure when he started to take notice of me, or if he was only taking notice of me cos I was taking notice of him, but either way, some weird connection had kicked off. There's a decent true crime section at the State Library and I spend a lot of time reading with my heart and soul about criminals, conmen, and fugitives of life. So when I saw him with the phonebook, aka *The Encyclopedia of Crime*, and taking notes, another layer was added. Soon we were surreptitiously, then not so surreptitiously, assessing each other's reading material, nodding approval, making our judgements. I got a bigger nod than usual when he saw me reading *A Sort of Life* by Graham Greene. It felt like I was at school trying to make friends with the cool kid, but the cool kid was a middle-aged man who wore plain-coloured casual outfits, had a confident gait, read widely, and one time was carrying an ancient copy of the *Egyptian Book of the Dead* around in a protective plastic folder.

So there I am, as usual, sitting in one of the forest-green chairs at one of the round tables in the Redmond Barry underneath the high ceilings reading a book called *On Killing* by ex-elite soldier and psychologist Dave Grossman. Essentially, it's about the psychological cost of learning to kill in combat and what it does to humans. It's a harrowing read. I'm thoroughly enjoying it. I'm interested in individuals who've been trained to kill. I want to know how much hectic shit the mind can endure. Meanwhile, a steady stream of traffic flows up the main highway of the library.

He appears as usual. Today he's wearing blue jeans, plain T-shirt, dark blue Adidas Gazelles, keeping it extra casual, with a plain-coloured jumper. Understated refinement. I look down as he looks at me. He walks by close enough to see what I'm reading. I catch a glimpse of his book, *Stick* by Elmore Leonard. He sits at a desk in the row with the plastic partitions that obscure half your head.

As is my custom, whenever I leave my spot to go to the toilet I grab a couple of massive books and put them with my stuff, to make it that little bit harder to steal the worthless-to-a-thief stuff that I have. If I haven't eaten my banana yet I'll put that there too. I do a quick check over in the plastic partition section and see that he's still there, safely obscured. I tend to use the disabled toilet if it's free. If anyone hassles me (in over a decade or more there's only been one time when I kept a woman in a wheelchair waiting) my reasons are sound and were further validated in that episode of *Curb Your Enthusiasm* when Larry David gets told off by someone for not being disabled when he emerges from the disabled toilet, and he replies he has a lisp and queries why one disability is considered legitimate, and something as potentially debilitating as a lisp isn't? I made my peace years ago. I get in and out no hassle. I'm on the way back, Buzzcut is walking out. The moment we've all been waiting for. He speaks first.

'How ya goin?'

He's got an old-school local accent that instantly transports me to my grandma Rose's sunroom in the western suburbs, and us kids are there, and Rose's partner Wally is there, wearing slacks and a white singlet, his hair brillcreamed back, drinking XXXX. Confronted with the fact that the man I'd respected and admired from afar is now right in front of me sounding like a memory of something so close to home, should've endeared me further, but I panicked. The interaction went something like this:

'How ya goin?'

My unthinking response:

'How ya goin?'

He smiled.

'You don't answer a question with a question.'

He was right and usually I wouldn't've. But instead of righting the ship, which is what I wanted to do, I went the other way, clicked into reptile mode.

'I don't tell people I don't know how I'm goin.'

Like I was a child and didn't talk to strangers. I've never said that to anyone in my life. I hated myself more with every second I stood there. And now that I'd said it, I had no choice. Closed shop on the cortex. He looked at me, insulted, which was my nonintentional intention. He laughed, a half joke on his face as though I was a fool. Looked right through me with his calm blue eyes.

'You're a dickhead.'

He walked away. What a disaster.

Post-library confrontation it was tense every time I saw him. A spiral opened quickly for us. It went from a lively aesthetic understanding and respect for the cut of each other's jib, to outright intimidation and borderline violent hostility. But I refused to make the situation bearable. I didn't alter my routine; neither did he. I wouldn't be defeated. Neither would he. It was now a game. Whoever averted their gaze first, lost. Adults in a staring contest. Reptiles on a rock. Yet if a day went by and I didn't see him, I was so relieved, I could've wept.

* * *

When a seriously crispy thief starts coming into the library, I lose my rhythm. I see him when he enters, moving so quietly that the junky crunch is audible. A tightly coiled hunter wearing three-quarter pants bunched up above the knee, knotted with the string pull cord. He's been coming into the library a few times a week to do the rounds. Today, he glides across the floor, arcs the perimeter, takes in the rows of desks, goes up the stairs and does the same thing. Pausing now and then near a desk, where an oblivious person has a handbag or a phone, before moving on. To get a better view, he flies up on to the railing, perches there for a bit, sweeps the floor with salivating eyeballs, then flies down and keeps moving. A few steps later, he's spotted an antelope calf struggling in the mud. He stops. I look around, but no-one else seems to see him. The student has her backpack slung over her chair. I'm on the lower floor looking up. He's got his side eye working overtime. Moves in. And just as the antelope's leg is bending double in the mud, she makes a startled gurgling noise of recognition; her study buddy appears, who notices the invisible junky. He disappears the very instant he becomes visible. Cover blown. I watch him ease down the stairs, arcing the opposite way, then he's gone. I've seen at least two wanted men and one wanted woman hanging out at the State Library at separate times. Fresh off *Crimestoppers*. It is a place for everyone, after all.

When I'm in the library I spend most of my time either A: seeking out antagonists, or B: being sought out by antagonists. Back then, I didn't know it was all one and the same. I don't see Buzzcut for a while, but that doesn't matter, cos there's no shortage of antagonists for me to engage with. My new antagonist is tall and serious, and wears sunglasses inside the library. The fact that I never see his eyes instigates the staring contest. We follow a similar pattern. One day I'm sitting down out the front and he comes out and we do the staring thing. But he's had enough. He beelines for me, aggressive strides, a flap of blue shirt loosens with the vigorousness of approach. He stops right in front of me. He keeps his glasses on. We're literally one metre apart. Me still seated. He's sweating, my heart is beating fast. Neither of us say a word. Cortisol pumping to knockout levels under our skin. He steps off. We continue as normal. Back inside, the junky is hunting again. Then Buzzcut comes back. And with my new established antagonist, I suddenly have a lot on my plate. I consider changing libraries. I do a session at City Library, but given its small size, and a shoeless old man's newspaper-rustling unapproachability, I only last a few days. I come back to where I belong, in the Redmond Barry.

The blast into granular oblivion can take place in the most prosaic of circumstances. I can be walking along the street, sitting on a bus, or standing on the steps of State Library Victoria, which is where I am now. December 2017 and the sun is out. A few minutes earlier I'd been working on some shit prose and got sick of how shit it was, and went out to join the world. But when I walked out into the sun and looked at all the people doing what people tend to do on warm days, it felt as though each surface, human or not, was bordered with a fine crystalline shimmer, sparkling in secret, like the illustrated borders of *The Eleventh Hour* by Graeme Base. Shimmering outlines around forest-green benches, around the chess pieces mid-game and around the brown hair and pink scrunchie of the European tourist who just secured victory. The more attention I paid to it, the brighter it got. It was like watching thousands of tiny bubbles on the underside of a submerged boat that, when breaking the surface every now and then, released its bubbles to the air, showering every surface with an HD-pixilated grit.

Seeing the borders of things shimmering like boat bubbles didn't mean much to me. I didn't know any different. The curvature of a pumpkin in the supermarket, or the nose of a dog. If the glow came every now and then, I didn't make a fuss. It felt good. Felt really good. Cos if it lasted longer than a few minutes, which happened often, there'd be an intense hyperarousal and hyperactivity, a two-step, and I'd get all juicy behind it. What would you do and where would you go if your reality suddenly became a wildly glistening absolute?

Autumn 2018. Cold grey day in Melbourne. I'm outside the library, under the sandstone awning, smoking a ciggy, taking a break, when I hear a scream and a slam from the entrance, rumpled footsteps, a thud. I look around as a young girl slides across the tiles. She's being dragged along the ground by the junky. She won't let go of her bag; neither will he, and it's all out in public and I'm right there. But I want him to be free, to make his escape. In daylight he looks much worse; he needs to be with other street hunters in a dark room with few distractions, not out here in the light. The girl is screaming and it's nasty to look when she goes bumping down the stairs with her arms above her head, twisting around like a clumsy torpedo. I feel guilty and change sides. But you can't out-desperado the most desperate; he yanks her bag off and she falls, yelling and pointing, her clothes torn, and now damp from the rain. I make a gesture to run. He turns and is gone, disappearing once more.

After the heat of commotion dies down, I feel how freezing it is out here. I pull my beanie lower on my head, zip up my jacket to my chin, squish my ciggy, and look at Swanston Street below. Cold air rips through wind tunnel tram stops with only plastic visors for cover. Dark coats pull close. A tram stops and a woman attempts to synchronise the opening of her orange umbrella as she steps off the tram, hoping to avoid all drops, but it's immediately blown inside-out like a jellyfish. A weak sun makes an appearance in a mediocre attempt at warmth, realises its mistake, quickly rectifies it. Such is the temperament of the city when it's miserable.

I didn't see Buzzcut for a long time, so long I think he's dead. But I always think people are dead when I don't see them for a while. Spring 2018. I'm waiting for documents, my police check, at the Flinders Street police station when I hear a voice I recognise. I look up. He doesn't see me cos I'm sitting to the right, far enough away from reception. I look away, then up sheepish, from an angle. It's Buzzcut:

'I wanna report something, make a complaint.'

The cop's eyes glaze.

'What's the nature of your complaint, sir?'

From his side profile, I see that there's not much of him, like he's been unwell.

'I live in Ascot Vale yeah and every time I do my laundry downstairs, I have to chase junkies out the laundry.'

'Ascot Vale, sir?'

'Yeah, the flats.'

'Did you report the matter to local police?'

'Yeah, they didn't do anything. And yesterday, I found a listening device in one of the washers.'

The cop asks him:

'Have you seen these individuals using drugs sir?'

'Course I have!'

'Ok, and this listening device, do you happen to have it with you?' Another cop appears, but not with my forms. He's got stripes. Looks at Buzzcut.

'No, I don't. I smashed it as soon as I found it.'

The cop with the stripes interjects.

'Sir, what we'll do is inform local police and some officers will attend the premises where this incident has taken place.'

Buzzcut gets out a pad and pen from his pocket and draws something, concentrates on the drawing, rips off the page, shoves it under the cops' noses.

'It looked like this.'

The cops share a look.

'Ok, sir.'

Another cop appears with my forms. I get up to grab them. I'm next to Buzzcut. I don't look at him. I get the forms, about turn, and glance down to see what he drew. He's drawn a sniper scope, in its crosshairs; a giant syringe.

3
Graff
The Writers' Reality

THE BUZZ

It's 1 am in 2004. I'm 18 years old. I'm solo under the bridge, halfway between North Melbourne and Spencer Street stations, the entry point to the CBD from the west, via Docklands. Behind me are wind tunnel landscapes and cheap-schmick towering apartment buildings. Thin glass beehives. Fire traps in waiting. I'm also a fire trap in waiting, crouched in front of the hole in the cyclone fence I just cut through with my mini-boltcutters the size of my forearm. The two trains are 50 metres across the tracks in front of me, with one carriage each under the bridge, protected from the rain. Cars blur past on the road down the slope behind me. It's midwinter and pouring rain. I'm sweating in my black Columbia jacket.

I check, double-check, triple-check my paint:

- 2 Dulux golds,
- 2 Dulux flat blacks,
- 1 Dulux sky-blue,
- 1 Belton white, and
- 1 Pastel Green Belton. Nozzles on.

The rain is comforting cos the security will be less willing to walk around the yard, unless they're hiding in the train, which they do, occasionally. I wait. And wait some more. I can see some of the brick wall of the remand centre on the other side of the train yard sprawl. I tighten my backpack straps so there's no room for the cans to bounce and make noise. Supple, subtle muscle when I move.

I step through the cyclone fence. To my right through hazy light is the low-hung box still called Spencer Street train station, before it got an undulating bubble for a roof. To my left are the snaking train tracks into North Melbourne station. The tiny suburb of West Melbourne starts above the tracks, runs from Festival Hall, up to the Vic Market, left down to the Royal Melbourne Hospital and inwards after a few blocks for the square. There's a place called Train Spotters lookout above the tracks in West Melbourne, on Railway Place, a sliver of a street lined with railway cottages. The Spotters lookout was designed by the local council back in the mid-1990s when local councils were making sculptures with incorporated elements of the landscape into their structure and placing them around the inner city. Bits of train parts, rusted metal, cyclone fencing, and concrete were joined together to form a platform that absorbs a panorama of grinding industry stretching out towards the horizon. Flickering lights, iridescent, working-class memories.

After looking left and right, I run across the tracks and make for a cosy little spot, back against a pillar, arm's length from the crinkled metal exterior of the train. Exposure time on the bolt, five or six seconds max. I open one of the train doors. I climb up into the empty carriage. It's a Connex train, dark blue exterior with yellow stripes through the blue. Similar colours inside, but with a lime-green splatter pattern on every seat. The rain-slicked shadows stretch and ripple through the silent train carriages like the environment is a dream, but it couldn't be more real. Heightened in the present. My nervous system floods with cortisol. There are six carriages each, and I walk them to the end, eyes on the swivel, checking out the carriages of the train next to it in case anyone's there, stopping every now and then to absorb sensory information, flickering in, flickering out. I do the same thing with the train next door.

Spencer Street yard is my favourite place to paint. There are only ever two trains at one time and when it rains, I get that rare feeling when painting a yard, a sense of security, albeit false, as rain doesn't deter the security guards. But the rain feels like protection, a guide, and of spiritual significance for an obsessive night-time kid like me. I ease open a train door and climb down. I settle in a perfect spot in the aisle on the gravelly walkway between the two trains and get to work.

Gold first. Then green around the gold to create a background. Black outline next and each letter comes into its own. The M takes shape, the O comes next, then the D. I add pastel-green background, strategic clouds, bubbles. Paint creeps up the window, fresh blotches, notches on the belt. I add touches of sky-blue to strategic spots on the pastel background, adding depth, then make it glow with a white final and white highlights. I'm done. I put my paint away. I step back, but as the train next to me is basically an arm's length away, I can't see that much, only from an angle. So I open the door of the train directly opposite, sit in the door, and tap a Peter Stuyvesant out of my soft pack, smoke, legs dangling.

I feel at home here; the wet lights and the drum of the rain on either side of me creates a wall of protection, time slowing down in the heat of the moment. I finish my ciggy, get out my disposable camera, take a few snaps. Lightning flashes in a cave. I put the camera away, run back across the tracks, climb through the hole in the fence, across the road, up and on to the bridge I was just under and walk as casually as I can back towards the CBD, turning left before the remand centre, in the direction of North Melbourne, through the rain.

SKATEBOARDING BECOMES GRAFF

Before I did Graff, like so many other kids, I was a skater. The place to be back then if you were a skater, or hung out in the scene, was the Sailyards, where the QV shopping complex now sits. Before it was Sailyards, it was the Queen Victoria Hospital.

The massive space was split in two, with the other half of the skatepark a vacant lot. The reason it was called the Sailyards was cos it had these big poles with flapping banners that were like sails. Everything was shabby and rugged, and the skatepark proper had rough red concrete that wore down your board and your shoes pretty quick. Older skaters cut that park up and I remember being in awe of them and the shit they could do: legends such as Will Stoyles, Jaffa Curtis, Jason Ridgeway and so many others. I learnt as much as I could from them. There were skate comps and all kinds of 1990s shit going on. The ramps were metal and hard, chipped wood. Eventually a YMCA hut was established in the skatepark to treat injuries.

At around 12 years old I got the first skateboard that wasn't a complete embarrassment from Kmart. It was a Christmas present. A stylish Habitat set-up. I hadn't begun stealing in earnest yet and had to wait for birthdays or Christmas if I wanted something brand new. So, I had the board, but I didn't have the fresh dope shoes to go with it; instead, I had an old pair of DCs shoes that I'd lathered in shoe goo (plastic concrete stuff), literally covering the whole front of the shoe cos I'd already torn through it.

At the back of the Sailyards was where the older boys used to hang out and drink and smoke. They'd be blasting music from a boom-box, wearing Ralph Lauren polo shirts and baggy jeans, Country Road sweaters, and I'd overhear them say how this was fresh, and that was fresh, and I'd be thinking about the Vic Market fresh produce section; it had nothing to do with that. I didn't know it then, but in amongst that crew of older skaters and city heads were some of the most original and prolific writers in the state.

SPOTSWOOD DRAINS

When I was 13–14 years old, I hung out with Anthony all the time. If we weren't riding around on bikes kicking over empty rubbish bins out the front of people's houses for fun after school, we'd go to Spotswood drains. George was Greek and lived with his mum and American stepdad, who he didn't get along with, in a new townhouse in a development right next to Cruikshank Park on the Yarraville/Kingsville border. The park down the street from Anthony's house had a creek running through the middle of it that started as a piss trickle in Sunshine, worked its way through Tottenham, then became a brook that babbled a bit when it hit the park, running over boulders that everyone used as a hopscotch bridge. Upstream from the boulder-cross was a willow tree with bobbing branches that were thick enough to grab hold of and swing over the waist-deep water and back to the bank.

The water became a thin channel, one metre across, as it cruised along behind the back fences of Kingsville, till the fences stopped and the walls opened up, as it reached the West Gate Bridge entry point, where eight lanes of traffic going in and out of the western suburbs converged above Williamstown Road. Buses bundled by directly overhead, towards the beach end of the inner west. The drains were tucked away in the armpit of the freeway turnoff, with Spotswood to the immediate right. Yarraville the immediate left. If you entered the slip lane and continued upwards to merge with the West Gate Bridge towards the city, and glanced downward, sharp left, you'd catch a glimpse of the 10ft-high concrete walls below.

It's a summer arvo and I'm down the drains with Anthony and we're throwing rocks, messing about, when we see three older guys, who would've only been in their early twenties walk into the drains, from the other side of Williamstown Road where the shitty golf course was. They were pointing at other pieces, smoking ciggies, drinking beers. They stopped about halfway along the drains, then motioned to where they would paint and began to unload spray can after spray can from their backpacks. We watched from a distance. After a little while, we edged closer, and soon we were close enough, on our side of the drain, to be within shouting distance.

At the start, it just looked like big blobs of shit and I couldn't understand why they'd want to come all the way down here to make big blobs of shit. But as they continued, their shapeless blobs became clean, highly stylised letters. I couldn't really read what the words said, so I asked one of them. The main guy in the middle with a beer and a ciggy, old tracksuit pants, loose polo shirt. He jolted his head at me and told me to fuck off ya dickhead, which I did, to a safe distance. Then we came back when they'd finished and went through the shit they left. But it was all trash. Just empty spray cans all over the place.

The next day me and Anthony rode our bikes to YENHOUT GIFTS in Footscray and stole a few $2 Export-brand cans and packets of sparklers to make sparkler bombs. Exports have a white chisel-tipped nozzle on a stem with a red square the size of chilli flake on it. Turning it clockwise gets you a flat spray. Then back again for a thin line. We racked two cans each. I had a black and a yellow, Anthony had a white and a chrome. I soon found out that the yellow was a watery see-through limp dick colour. Disappearing as soon as it appeared. The black was better. We both picked words like INSANE or KRAZY and emptied the cans on the walls. But daytime tagging was lame. So we planned to go to the drains at night. We coordinated the classic, I'm staying at Anthony's, Anthony is staying at mine.

Earlier that day we went to a different $2 store in Footscray and stole more cans. I got everything ready at home, packed my bag. In my head we were preparing for war, but the enemy turned out to be two lime-greens and two yellow exports. I thought that two layers would do the trick, but it became two layers of watery shit instead. Anthony, next to me, with his hair gelled for the occasion, suffered a similar defeat. We had to stop. No more paint. We left the drains and chose Anthony's house, as my mum was hypervigilant.

At the time my family lived in Yarraville, two minutes from the Werribee and Williamstown train line, the Spotswood Golf Course, and the murky backwater slush under the Westgate, before it washed out into the shipping channels of the Yarra River. The train sliced through the industrial run-off, brothel carparks and operational factories, a train bridge over the slush. There was a little spot tucked away in the overpass of that bridge, a spot just big enough for me – I just had to kick out a family of pigeons. I stashed paint and smoked ciggies there. The trains rumbling, literally, right over me, my whole body shaking. As soon as it got dark, I'd take my cans and walk along the train line from my spot to Yarraville train station, tagging on the back fences. Hiding when the trains passed, their yellow interiors flickering over me in the dark. When I changed schools, I saw Anthony less.

TOTTENHAM FREIGHT YARD
When we moved from Yarraville into a small weatherboard in Footscray in 2001 it meant that Tottenham freight yard was only two train stations away, and I started going there to do tags and walk around by myself all the time. Totty Yard housed company-green freights with a yellow infinity symbol painted on their side, alongside other cylindrical grey- and brown-speckled freights, and most of them travelled from Tottenham all around Australia, before coming back home to rest. The yard itself stretched from West Footscray Station past Tottenham and halfway towards Sunshine. On the stretch, past West Footscray on one side, was all factories and houses behind them, and just before Tottenham Station was a newsagent, a bottle shop and a fish and chip shop. My dad's aunt Patty lived near Tottenham Station, and before we moved to Yarraville we went over to their house. It was memorable cos Patty had gotten a bucket of KFC 24-piece feed for the occasion, and my mum, who'd never let us eat KFC, had to watch me and my brother feast on the chicken.

Years later, with a can of paint instead of a drumstick, I'm in the yard, walking across the tracks that were lit up by these looping lights connected from pole to pole above, and it was kinda cinematic, cos you had the whole yard to yourself and the smoky glow from the lights would catch the paint from the pieces on the big grain movers, all lit up in the dark. I don't know what it was about going out to paint solo at night but there was a spiritual quality to it. Maybe it had something to do with owls? I've had a painting of an owl above my bed since I was a child, and it's still there. Staring out blankly at everything. But it turned out that my solo Graff night vibe had nothing to do with owls at all. Night missions are good for the imagination, good for alertness, and were good practice for slowly developing aggressiveness, building via numerous factors, location-specific, innate, implanted there to flourish like a virus, undetected. Unconscious prep for all those high-gloss, low-self-esteem, night-time achievements in the future.

In 2002 I got expelled from Lynall Hall Community School for gouging my tag into the metal front door of the brand-new school, but when I got the boot, it was perfect cos now I could become utterly dedicated to Graff. Even though I was still a toy, by sheer activity, I forced myself on Melbourne. It was everything to me, took up all my time, consumed all my energy, 24/7, 365-days-in-my-bones-obsession.

TOOLS OF THE TRADE

Running loops and doing insides with my 15ml marker was one of my favourite things to do. I'd get on the back carriage of a train and sweep through it, hitting strategic spots on the way. I might sit down and do an upside-down tag on the underside of a seat. If it was a Hitachi, I'd pull down the window, lean out and get busy hitting the outside and, if it was particularly quiet, I'd sit in the window proper, legs in, while reaching up and out to the top to hit the roof of the train with my right hand, while holding on to the raised ridged train roof border with my left.

The 15ml felt-tipped marker was initially a glue pen that I racked in bulk from Priceline and converted to a marker afterwards. They were easy to rack cos they were small and compact, and the big Priceline stores, like the one that used to be on the third floor of an arcade in the CBD, were mostly empty. Once racked, it was washed, refilled with heavy-duty stain, then taped up with masking tape. In those days I always had ink stains on my belly and my balls from where I kept my marker in my jocks. Ink stains on my hands. Ink stains in my clothes. Ink stains in the layers of skin. Sometimes I'd wear gloves when making a stain for a marker; other times, I'd forget.

Getting the right ingredients that would produce the most toxic stain was the goal, so that when it was buffed on the inside of the train, the ink would act as a paint stripper, eat into the essence of the structure to leave its mark there once the top layer had been scrubbed away. Luckily, the main ingredient that goes into a marker to produce the darkest stain was a specific ink called Blacktop, and through the Graff grapevine we all ended up going to a specific newsagents on Smith Street in Collingwood where it was sold. I wonder how many teenagers legitimately needed bottles of ink. It was a nice little earner. A single small bottle was $5 in the early oughts. You couldn't steal it cos they put it behind the counter. The other main ingredient was acetone, in nail polish remover, and I could steal bottles of that from anywhere.

I was willing to travel long distances if I got word of an unsuspecting shop that sold inks or dyes that added depth and toxicity to the stain. I remember being the only person on the local bus in Eltham in the morning as it made its way through an industrial area. And when I asked the driver to drop me off between some factories, he checked to see if I was lost. I wasn't. I found it, but the info was only half right. It was a semi-warehouse specialising in horse-riding equipment, and they did have dyes, but not for general sale. If you knew a rack that hadn't been done too much and it happened to be out the middle of nowhere, then out in the middle of nowhere you'd go. Other times, it was a trip to Collingwood. I only paid for what was physically impossible to steal, like Blacktop ink and high-quality 'paint' and if you got your start on the westside like I did, and you needed paint, the place to go back then was called VA's, now called GIANT, in North Melbourne.

VA's was basically invisible. A brick-fronted building on the hill on Dryburgh Street, that even if you walked past the steps leading inside, you wouldn't see anything. It was set up like a cave. Up the steps and to the left was a locked door with a buzzer and a grille that the owner, a Graff head, would open after sizing you up. Once inside, depending on how busy it was, you either went straight into where the paint was, or kicked back in the low-roofed, black-painted waiting room with a wall dedicated to tags. It was in that tiny room where the imagination went to work, where reality and myth combined. The fact that you were following the same path of a living legend who left his mark where you did, a kid hungry to learn, was like getting close to God.

Cos I got my start in Graff in the West I was influenced, stylistically, regarding letter construction, by writers who came from the area. And the main guy was a writer who wrote DUKE, CKA who, by 1996, was already a legend. And by the time I came to Graff, he was the best of the best. A true innovator. The other three were RUNS, CKA, TSF, TCB, a heavy hitter from St Albans. Then, a legend who wrote SPOTEM, CKA, TSF, from out west. Also someone closer to my age, a writer from Werribee, now dead, who wrote KERTAN, TPS. There were others too, but I can trace a specific style I was developing from my admiration and respect for those four writers and how they went about it.

VA's stocked top-of-line quality paint that mostly came from Germany and other parts of Europe. Brands with names like *Montana* and *Belton*. The paint room was arm-span-width across with shelves stacked with cans on all sides. The old head never took his eyes off you. I still managed to rack, but only on a handful of occasions. The cans at VA's were the opposite of Export cans. No built-in stem. The onus was on you to make the right choice for what you were doing. A New York fat cap produces the fattest blast of paint and sounds like a machine piston under the index. Crinkle-cut texture with an orange circle. A pink dot was a hooded cap, low down, less brash, not as fat, but still chunky. Then blue dots, basically one size down from pink. Then black dots, small-size spray for more delicate work. Then they get thinner, gold dots. Some other dots I can't recall. Throughout the years I was writing, I only really used three nozzles. Fat, medium and small. Different nozzles for different activities.

VA's was for high-end cans only; the rest, like Dulux cans, were racked almost into extinction cos the paint shops that stocked them didn't keep them behind the counter. Plastikotes were mid- to high-end cans with a vast colour range, also racked relentlessly. In the Graff ecosystem there are writers who steal and writers who don't. I was the former. Historically, kids who did Graff didn't have any money, and even if you did, the last thing you spent it on was paint. Writers who didn't rack were immediately under suspicion.

For young men looking for masculine expression, Graff had it all, and even though it was all a deeply fragile, anti-developmental, addiction-incubating backward claustrophobic headfuck, everybody needs a rite of passage, right?

THE HEIDELBERG SPECIAL

It's autumn in 2002 and I'm waiting near the entrance to Footscray Station for the Flinders Street train. While I wait, I suss out the 4ft-high, hollow plastic triangle that provides commuters with the latest information relating to crime committed on public transport. A photo of the offender, a description of the offence. I never missed a chance to see who was doing what, and where. They used to be at major train stations, but they've taken most of them away. Back then, 75 per cent of crime in the plastic was graffiti-related and cos Graff was my full-time job, sussing it out was like reading the daily news.

The train comes. I get on. I'm on my way to meet Frank. He's got short black hair, grey-blue eyes, and always wore a big Nike jacket. We'd become close friends at Lynall Hall Community School, and when I got expelled earlier that year, he just wagged school to hang out with me. Frank lived in a residential care unit in Preston, behind the Maccas, which at the time I thought was great. He had his own room and the only time I ever saw an adult was when the worker came by at around 8 pm to do the obligatory knock. The worker would knock on the door, ask if he was ok, Frank would tell him he was, and that was that. Didn't even open the door. And there wasn't another round till morning. We smoked bongs, listened to Necro and Ill Bill, sketched in his books, then we'd go out for a bomb, depending on how high we were.

Most mornings we'd link up at Flinders Street, like we do today, hanging around the train station like a couple of mini-trainspotters on the lurk. Although we outright avoid the actual trainspotters, a deep geek misfit crew that congregated down the Spencer Street end of Platform Two. The leader of the misfits was a morbidly obese middle-aged man with a small head, short black hair, parted, who was always leaning on one of the maroon and yellow handrails to support his body, forearms crossed, gazing at the trains. His sidekick was a thin, ferrety guy with an enormous moustache; he was always writing stuff in his big notebook, dates, times, types of trains.

The Heidelberg Special was always a Hitachi train, and it ran express from Flinders Street to Clifton Hill, then express again to Heidelberg. It was fourteen train stations to Heidelberg, but it only stopped twice. Once at Clifton Hill, six stations from Flinders Street, then at Heidelberg, end of the line, eight stations later. Between Flinders and Clifton Hill was where we went to work. The Heidelberg special was at 10 am, and by that time peak hour had slowed to a trickle.

We get on the empty back carriage and wait till the train leaves Flinders Street, and as it goes through the first tunnel, we begin. Soon, black ink is dripping juicily down the white surfaces. Stations whoosh past. We've gone from one end of the first carriage to the next, walked through the doors of the second carriage, and are halfway down. An announcement over the loudspeaker. I freeze mid seat straddle. Lock eyes with Frank, crouching near a door.

'You've been observed vandalising the train. The police have been notified.'

OK, so the train's gone through Vic Park station and isn't slowing down. It pulls into Clifton Hill Station and is coming to a stop. By now, Frank and I are at the back door at the end of the last carriage, and I've got my foot on the handle to force it as it slows down. A divvy van speeds past parallel to the station. The last carriage pulls in. And as it slows, I force the door; it beeps as Frank goes under my leg and kinda falls, but the train is almost stopped now, so he's ok. I jump out and see the blue and green cop vests flash colour in the peripheral. We run the other way, jump down on to the tracks behind the train and keep running. The two cops struggle on to the tracks. Our head start saves us. We disappear down a side street and over a back fence next to the train line. We land in some bushes and stay quiet. Sitting on the dirt, up against the inside of the fence, we're spoilt for adrenaline. We have a ciggy. The ciggy tastes good.

A week later I'm at Clifton Hill. I've got my cap low and a collared shirt on. I pass the plastic triangle. Fuck me, there we are! Frank and me. Wanted for criminal damage. An image of us taken from a CCTV camera at the end of platform where we jumped down, running towards freedom. I look closer. I didn't have my cap on that day, just a jacket that zipped up over half my face. My clothes relatively non-descript, but you can make out the Nautica symbol on my navy-blue jacket. Frank's face is clearly visible, very identifiable. He gets taller every time I see him. I pull my cap low, head down, paranoid, but there's no-one around at 11 am on a Tuesday. The train comes. I get on; it's mostly empty. I find a window seat and start smiling like I've just won the gold. The recognition, the solidarity, the respect from my peers will come.

We made it! But made what? Back then, I didn't have a clue why I *really* did what I did. That level of self-awareness wasn't available, and even today it's still blurry. I guess it's odd to think that getting my picture on a tiny Crimestoppers notice at a train station could've filled me with such pride. Maybe it's like other passions where the risk vs reward equation is heavily skewed toward risk, like those people who climb hectic mountains. There must be a blind spot as to why someone would be so in love with something that has such potential to injure and ruin. Maybe operating in the extreme present tense is the juice of it. The air you breathe at that altitude, whether snow-capped high or all the way down low, does strange things to the mind and body. Primal, precipice-close. Alive.

INNER WEST TO SOUTHEAST

In 2003 when I was 17, my mum, dad and I moved from Footscray to a crumbly art deco flat in Elsternwick. My older brother moved out and we three moved in instead. It didn't take long to connect with a batch of local writers.

The first time I hung out with Daniel he got capsicum-sprayed outside a servo by two cops who had warrants out for his arrest, then thrown into the back of a divvy van. Daniel was a stocky Russian Jew who lived in a mansion in Caulfield. His tag was MACHO (I didn't think anything of his choice of tag at the time). He'd started a crew and chucked me in. CDP had three meanings: Crime Drugs Power, Crim Damage Posse and Crime Does Pay. I loved crime. I loved drugs and I enjoyed the power I could wield on the general public. Daniel set the benchmark high. He was in and out of jail all the time.

Daniel's chaotic energy was at its peak in his destruction of the Jolimont Wall. A 100-metre-long stretch of wall just past Richmond Station on the MCG side. It was painted an institutional blue-grey colour, a dead palette, and sat in the middle of the train tracks, exposed, and it was on that stretch of wall, back in the early oughts, that Daniel came to life.

The first time I saw his trademark approach to damage, I was going past it on the train. And as the train ran parallel to it the wall had changed colour from blue to black, by Daniel doing literally hundreds of individual tags from the top to the bottom, across the whole length of it. It was an unbelievable sight. For anyone not in the Graff game it was just vandalism, but to me, it was legendary. And the brazenness. There were only a few writers who did damage like Daniel did, but they did most of it north of the city. Daniel was a fresh scumbag, a CDP scumbag. He did the Jolimont Wall the same way over and over and again. They'd paint over it, and that was his call to action. Back he'd go. Until he got caught. But even getting pinched didn't stop him. Back he'd go. Get arrested. Get out of jail and go back to Jolimont Wall, returning to the scene of the crime. Daniel also had a party trick, which was to get inside the driver's compartment at the end of the train, then essentially act as a hijacker by commandeering the train's loudspeaker and saying the train had been taken over by terrorists. Daniel's deep voice would boom through the carriages. People scrambled to escape, forced doors, climbed out windows.

Sam was a wild kid. When he was 15 years old, he went up to South Australia to get his motorcycle licence, jumping the queue by two years. He rode around town on a Ducati 999 Superbike in a pair of shorts and a T-shirt. Sam was the youngest brother of three. His older brother Jarod, closer to my age, was a livewire too. His oldest brother Bryan was straight as an arrow. Their dad wasn't around. The three brothers lived with their mum in Caulfield. Sam's tag was KASH.

Shawn was a ladies' man. He lived in Ormond; his dad owned a plumbing business, and he was an apprentice. He had a car and a job. Shawn was the most stable out of all of us. Emotionally mature, a good listener. Shawn wrote CADET. We were all in CDP, plus a few more guys, and very active in the inner southeast, the inner city, northwest and west, from 2002/3 onwards.

Sam and I were so competitive that we didn't paint together anywhere near as much as we could've. And the few times we did panels together, I was annoyed at how mine turned out. A lot of my panels were small, and he'd always bag me about it. I have a photo of me that Sam took when a few of us were doing panels at Burnley yard, at around 3 am in winter 2004. Sam had already finished his, so he snapped a pic of me as I was doing the finishing touches on mine. In the pic I'm reaching up as far as I can, and I barely reach the windows. I'm wearing a thick grey fleece and one of those beanies with earflaps and pom-poms on the end, the sort of thing I'd never wear during the day in public, and I look like a daggy child. But even though I was embarrassed about the pom-pom earflap beanie, I liked the pic. I think he did too. We both had a lot of respect for each other but it was hard to really show it. That night, I rode in the boot of the car, as there were too many of us. In those days, I literally walked around with the short straw in my pocket.

MISSIONS

I didn't have my driver's licence and neither did most of my friends, so sometimes we'd catch a NightRider bus to the train yards. One time

I went from the city out to Hurstbridge with a friend, Lil Chris, who I spent heaps of time with back in the day. We had bags full of paint and were meeting a few others out there. Hurstbridge is like a country town. We were there to do panels. We got off the bus like a couple of tourists. The guys we were meeting were there, and they'd brought one of their friends I didn't know. We went and hid in some bushland, waiting 50 metres away from where the trains were fenced in.

We were waiting in an enclosed rocky overhang type thing, with big gum trees all round and stars bunched close and clean through the leaves, scurrying animals, night noises. I'm a city kid, I didn't like the bush at night all that much. But the most annoying thing was the kangaroos. The big motherfuckers would pop up near us, silvery ears all pointy and twitchy in the light. We were in their spot, but they left us alone, and we obviously did likewise. Finally, we got set, cut through the fence, and got underway. The four of us painting one carriage, end to end. I heard footsteps that sounded like slippers on the concrete. Soon we saw slippers at the front gate; we were near the back, so we ran out the way we came, back to our spot in the bush. We watched the yard from there.

An old guy wearing a dressing gown and slippers appeared, looking like he was sleepwalking, casually strolling through the train yard. Turned on a train and got in. He had a thermos. He opened it and settled in, as familiar as if it was his kitchen. Then just sat there. He didn't walk to the back, and he wasn't in any rush. Just hanging around. We were fucked. Not gonna happen now. We got a lift outta there with the others. I found out later that the driver lived next door to the yard.

Cold nights in high grass near Upfield train station waiting for the first train in the morning. Chased by police dogs. Shivering through winter nights watching security guards do their rounds. Absolute dedication. On the NightRider again, this time to Belgrave where I got drunk and passed out on the way. Woke up when I was thrown out into the aisle as the bus jolted to a stop. My friend in hysterics.

OLD MATE WITH PAINT CANS IN BRIEFCASE

It was 7:30 am some time in 2004 when I got off the train at Moorabbin train station. I didn't take any notice of the nondescript white guy in his late 20s wearing a suit, carrying a briefcase, walking a few dozen paces ahead of me, who disappeared into a cul-de-sac. I turned in to the same quiet cul-de-sac, with brick units and trimmed lawns. I'd gotten up at 6:30, taken the tram from Elsternwick up Glenhuntly Road to Glenhuntly Station, got on the train with commuters, off at Moorabbin to then walk through the suburban backstreets to where the train would lay up on a curved section of track on the residential side, going towards Frankston.

At the end of the cul-de-sac there's a thick line of bushes, then a wooden fence and the train line, where the empty train is supposed to stop. I walk past the bushes a few times to find the easiest way in. As I'm searching for a gap, I hear a voice from inside the bushes.

'Get in or you'll get spotted.'

I don't hesitate. I jump in the bushes and almost knock over the guy with the briefcase. He's annoyed. And reluctantly introduces himself, and his tag, STAN. A very active train painter with 70K crew. He tells me how the layup works. I'm proud that this weirdo in a suit with his paint cans in a briefcase will let me do a panel with him. The intensely hierarchical structure of Graff means that I instantly respect him, no question. We wait, the train comes, pulls up right where it's supposed to, but leaves after thirty seconds. STAN, the semi-balding IT vibe guy with the panel nous.

'It's like that sometimes. Anyway, catch ya kid.'

He climbs over the fence and disappears. And I wonder if he's off to his other job, working in a call centre or something. That briefcase schtick is a good move.

Graff-heads are either getting up when the working day begins to get shit done or coming home at the same time after being up all night painting. Shift work for no money. Just glory. Grimy and stinking, exhausted in a four-seater on a packed train carriage at 9 am. Or dressed crisp and clean on the way to a suburban layup. If you don't have tunnel vision and an almost myopic approach to the world, then you won't succeed in Graff.

The level of commitment to the lifestyle means that addiction is part and parcel for so many writers. It's one of the reasons why so many writers have substance abuse issues, cos so much of the lifestyle is flooded with dopamine. And there's no class distinctions. All that matters is, you're either a toy and don't rack or you're a thief and are fresh. Petty crime and addiction usually go hand in hand. The heightened, insular nature of that world is also a good place to hide out, especially if there's hectic subconscious pain in your soul. Graff has a habit of letting unearthed ruin run express towards absolute derailment, clearing the path, making sure that inevitability occurs faster, and the compartmentalisation becomes so extreme that you no longer know how to exist outside of Graff. I'm not an apathetic individual, far from it. But if you asked me who the prime minister of Australia was in the early oughts, I would've had to look it up.

SAM'S FUNERAL

It's 2010. I'm 25. I get a call from a number I don't recognise. I hadn't been involved in Graff for a few years, and I'd lost touch with old mates. It's Shawn, CADET. Calling to invite me to a funeral.

'It's Sam. He's dead.'

I hadn't seen Sam, aka KASH, for years. I'd heard about the horrific motorbike accident he'd been in a few years ago. He'd lost the use of his legs and was in a wheelchair as a result. Shawn is crying. I think it and say it out loud:

'He must've been in so much pain.'

Sam's Facebook was an image of him hand-gliding in Brazil in a wheelchair – Sam still being Sam.

'Fuck man. How old was he?'

'23.'

I think about his brothers, his mum. How messed up, how hard it would be for them. I ask after Jarod, the middle brother and the one I knew.

'He's been in jail for a few years now, armed robbery I think.'

'Really?'

'Yeah, was around the same time of Sam's motorbike accident.'

The healthy competitive energy and pure heart that Sam brought to life was incomparable. I mean, it's not like one able-bodied person is more suitable for a wheelchair than another, but I doubt many people had such a movement-based approach to everything as Sam did. Irrepressible, fucken boundless. Shawn and Sam were close.

'How are you holding up, man?'

'Pretty terrible aye can't stop crying.'

Shawn will have a son and name him Sam.

I drive from Brunswick to Kooyong and get to the funeral home late. I couldn't find the entrance. It was up a winding road in lush garden surrounds. I park and walk up the incline to the top where the service was being held. The first person I see is Adam, aka FATSO. I didn't recognise him at all. He's leaning against a car, wearing a black suit and Versace sunglasses. When I knew him, he was a massive 6ft-3 pimply kid who delivered wildly entertaining insults and jokes in rapid-fire patter.

During Christmas and New Year back in 2006/07, Adam and an unidentified co-accused put on balaclavas and waited in a park to rob a guy of $2000 worth of drugs. Adam had a double-barrel shotgun; his mate had a meat cleaver. Adam fired a shot into the air to show the dealer they were serious. Adam was arrested within 24 hours. He was charged with three counts of attempted armed robbery, intentionally cause serious injury, possessing an unregistered firearm, common assault, trafficking a drug of dependence, and possessing a drug of dependence. He was sentenced to a five-year prison term. He had no prior criminal convictions. A psychologist, a Mr Joblin, noted in his report that the appellant Adam had 'an extremely fatuous and child-like presentation and believing that he belonged to an environment that demanded demonstrations of serious criminal activity, he thus, in an extremely childlike manner, participated in these offences'.

Today at the funeral, there's not an ounce of fat on Adam, virtually unrecognisable from my memories of him five years ago. Hair short, gel spiked. A thin pallbearer at a gangster's funeral. He takes off his glasses and smiles, and it's a relief to hear he's still got the trademark cheekiness.

'It's little Modzy n shit, how are ya?'

I overdo my grip strength when I shake his hand.

'Hey man. Long-time-no-see. Lookin good! Nice suit.'

I feel underdressed, too casual in shirt and jeans. After that, I don't really know what to say to him. I add:

'It's so fucked up about Sam.'

Then I see Jacob, aka MARIO, a good friend of mine from back then. From Carrum Downs, a few train stations from Frankston, Jacob lived in a brick unit with his mum and a blindingly white malamute pup. I never saw his dad. Jacob was a silly kid full of game-playing slyness, gullible. He had brown skin, black hair and brown eyes. Tall and handsome. We went to Caulfield Community School together. He still looks the same, the big brown eyes darting about, sorta anxious, always ready for silliness, more serious today.

'Dom, how ya been?'

'Yeah, all right man.'

His eyes do the Mario shuffle, and instantly I see the Jacob I remember. Us climbing over the fence at Caulfield Community, the school I went to after Lynall Hall, to have one last go at high school, to wag, catching trains together. Rorts, beach, Graff, girls and parties.

Jacob tells me it's an open casket and it's about to close so if I wanna see him I better go now. I say I should go see him, but when I go in the coffin has literally just been closed and I don't really know what to do. I go over and look at the closed box, feeling stupid, self-consciously aware that I'm looking at a closed coffin, and shameful at thinking of myself, unable to block out the background noise in my head, so I can be here in the moment. I ought to do something, so I reach out and place my palm on the pine, where Sam's face would be. I take my hand away. I'm relieved when the funeral director, a middle-aged, pearled blonde woman, announces for us all to come in.

Faces foreground and background, blur in and out. Jacob, Adam and then I go to the back right-hand corner and group together. Then I see Shawn; he comes over, and we hug. Sam's friends I don't know fill up the chapel. A projector and screen are turned on above the coffin. One of Sam's friends takes the stand. A slide show begins. Then Shawn gets up to do his speech, clumsily delivering anecdotes. Tells a short one.

'I remember when me, Sam and Dom would ride the trains and open the windows and spit on people's backs on the way out the station.'

After the service, Jarod, Sam's brother, appears, flanked by two plain-clothes cops. A jacket draped over his handcuffed hands. He's been allowed out for his brother's funeral. Jarod is bombarded with well wishes from all angles. I step in and shake his hand, brief eye contact.

We go to the wake at a friend's house and eat and drink. A mate approaches and he hands me a photo of Sam. He's smiling, a little white flower behind his ear. Tanned, taken in Bali. Attached is Sam's name and RIP in Graff-font. It's a sticker that peels off. A couple hours later we say our goodbyes. Adam tells me to come and hang out with him and Jacob soon, and I agree. He gets in his black Mercedes with Jacob, and they leave. I get in my early 90s Nissan Pintara wagon and drive back across the city. I stick the RIP Sam sticker on my bedroom window when I get home.

A SERENDIPITOUS OUT

I definitely wouldn't have used the word serendipitous to describe the decision of the judge presiding over my final court case in 2006, but thinking on those years I very easily could've joined the damned. I wasn't young any more. I was twenty years old. By then, I'd been to children's court three separate times. And magistrate's court four times, all for petty matters. There didn't seem to be much escalation in my offending, it was more about the accumulation over the last two years, in four separate appearances:

- 1 x behave in offensive manner in public
- 1 x criminal damage (intent damage/destroy)
- 1 x trespass on land owned by authority/corporation
- 1 x wilfully damage property
- 3 x theft charges
- 1 x deal in property suspected proceed of crime

The magistrate's assessment of what to expect from the trajectory of my criminal behaviour completely took me off guard. He'd seen enough young men like me to predict where I would end up and what my life would be like if I kept going the way I was. When the judge saw me smirk, it was a move that brought wrath to his speech, so much so that he removed his bridge-of-the-nose-spectacles and unleashed. Telling me that I better get ready to fight cos that smirk is gonna get wiped off in jail. I went pale and forgot where I was. He let me wobble and stay pale, then after the longest 30 seconds of my life, he continued, saying he was recording a conviction against me. I got my colour back. He made me think I was going to jail after his remarks, and it scared the shit outta me.

In court that day, a perfect storm opened up and I was given a choice. A choice that so many young men and women don't get, or if they do, their circumstances make it incredibly difficult to shift gears. After that court appearance I moved down to Wonthaggi with my parents, worked two jobs for a year, did a few rorts here and there, and saved money to buy a plane ticket to London. I was gone for a year. And I had 12 months to see what happened when I was not up to my neck in everything petty-crime-related.

DEAD. IN JAIL. DRUG ADDICTION

Two months after I saw Frank at the funeral, he killed himself, by gunshot. Apparently, he'd been smoking so much ice he'd become psychotic. Another story was he'd also ripped off some Vietnamese heroin dealers and they were out to get him, and instead of them getting him, he got himself. The words of Frank's lawyer quoting the psychologist when he tried to appeal his sentence splash in my mind, like when we used to jump off the bridge into the sea over the channel at Carrum Downs overpass.

I heard nothing from Jacob for many years after I saw him, then some CCTV footage that went nationwide popped up. In it, Jacob is riding down a street in Frankston on a bike. He gets off and goes into a gun shop, opens a cabinet, removes a rifle, and puts the rifle in a green bag with half of it poking out. Before jumping back on the bike and riding away. He served three years and is now an ice junky. Frank is in and out of jail. Daniel went to jail for three years and spent time in the Acacia Unit in Port Philip Prison for starting riots. Jarod, Sam's older brother, got out of jail a couple of years ago, and died of an overdose. Two out of three brothers dead. Shawn is the only person from that era who's doing well, and me, sort of.

Graff, for all its intense beefs and fights over where, what, and who, welcomes any and all wanderers, searchers, kids looking for connection, love, and brotherhood but in the end, getting in deep most likely means you won't get out, and if you do, you'll end up trapped in one of life's backwaters not knowing how you got there, or how to get out.

THE URGE RETURNS

I was in my late 20s and had nothing left to prove when, for some reason, an enormous white billboard on top of a 12-storey building on Flinders Street live-wired old inklings and became something I had to paint. I hadn't done a piece in years, which was a big risk, given how exposed the spot was. If I fucked up, it faced the trainline. The harshest critic.

The building itself was 90 per cent residential. The first floor was old retail, a shoe store, an Indian restaurant, apartments inward-facing in an open cylindrical box. A shabby indoor water fountain as centrepiece. Red brick, rusted-iron walkways, subcontinental languages from open doorways, washing lines threaded through fence railings. Massive skylight above. A wonky lift took me to the top floor, then the fire escape on to the roof, empty beer bottles, ashtrays. I looked at the back of the billboard, and how it was suspended on a metal structure that I would have to climb. There was one metre of space to walk in front of the billboard, then 12 stories down.

I came back that night and went into the Indian restaurant. The only reason for being in the building was to go to the average restaurant, or cos I lived there. Paranoid. I ate some of a dry samosa with a glass of water at a tiny table to see if anyone paid any attention to me. They didn't. I took the rest of the samosa in a bag, nibbled it, then chucked it in a bin. I went to the lift and up to the top floor, back through the fire escape and out on to the spongy surfaced roof that was like a giant rotting gym mat. I was wearing shorts, long-sleeve top and a cap. It was nearly the end of summer. My backpack with paint strapped tight.

I jumped up and grabbed one of the supporting poles supporting the billboard, wrapped my legs around it and shimmied up. At the top of the pole I swung around, keeping my body tight and close to the right-hand corner of the board, and up and on to the metal walkway. There was wind, but not too much. I walked from one end to the other, crouched down and opened my bag. I had a mad view from here, above the city. The trains went past on the bridge about 50 metres below. I could see tiny people through the train windows. Green light glowing from within as it clacked along the tracks. I looked out over the edge of the building, down at the mid-week nightlife at the King Street end of the city. Basically empty.

I painted with my nose about 15 cm away from the white canvas material. It was hard to get spatial awareness and I felt like a miniature person perched on the nose of a massive, empty white face. I stopped, looked left and right, diagonally up to each point of the board. I made bad choices with my colour selection, using chrome on white, black was ok, but orange for background was a dud move, and about halfway through all I wanted was to finish, and to be back down on the street. Finally, I was done. I climbed down the pole on to the roof, flooded with the familiar feeling. An energy that dilated my pupils and made me wanna chain-smoke ciggies. I was hungry. I should've saved the other half of that samosa. In the lift and out on to the street, with that nice buzz, thinking about tomorrow and how it would look in the daytime. In the end, not that great.

4
Grey Metallic Blue

The faces of my family are circling me like searchlights in the ocean. Earlier, I'd been drifting on a raft made of oil drums tied together with coconut palms, and a few old skateboards for a base. My hat caught water to drink. I also used the hat to trap a bird for food but when I looked at the bird's tiny black opal eye, it was CCTV from the sky, and I refused to eat robotics. I shooed it away. I'd been paddling on the open ocean for some time. My sail made of a long sheet of plastic tarp. I'd drawn a Nautica symbol on it in case any other boys on rafts saw it so they'd know I was part of their tribe. Eventually, the people behind the searchlights came into focus. I open my eyes in the trauma ward.

My parents and older brother are here. Mum looks like she's aged considerably, as though three decades chased her down in one night. I've only ever seen my dad cry once, at his mother's funeral. They lean over the bed to inspect me, faces anguished, smudged tired from a sleepless night. My brother's wearing rave clothes, looks like he came straight from a dance floor. Mat, once a close friend who'd become a drugs-only friend at some point, is so uncomfortable, I want him to go. I can move my thumb just enough to press the morphine buzzer in my right hand.

* * *

At around 2 am in the middle of summer last year, two weeks shy of my thirty-second birthday, I took a running jump off the balcony on the third floor of a friend's flat. I used my upward-bounding momentum to jump up and over the waist-high concrete barrier with plants on it where I often stood to rest my drink and smoke a cigarette. The drop took about two seconds. I hit the ground and ragdolled like one of those cylindrical blow-up car yard mascots. I landed hands-first like I was trying to sit down on a chair, thinking that I would break the fall that way. Shattered both wrists and fractured nearly all of my fingers. They had to be snapped back into place in the ED while I was juiced to the gills on ketamine. My right wrist had to have wires put in to help rebuild the bone that had crumbled like a stepped-on shell. Fractured pelvis, smashed right eye socket, and a jaw broken in three places. I was unconscious for a long time while blood pooled around my head like a murder scene. Apparently, if you fall from eight metres or more it's a fifty-fifty chance of survival. I was a complete mess, but I was alive.

(I)

The hospital walls in the trauma ward are a grey metallic colour, not quite grey, not quite blue, not quite anything. On the walls, there's suspicious-looking stains that look like they're from inside the body, and my imagination takes flight as I home in on the years of human scunge. If I stare long enough at the subliminal fluid collage on the wall at the foot of my bed, it becomes one of those 3D puzzle things, the answer rising out of it. There's also an A4-sized whiteboard with my name, my injuries, what I'm allergic to, and what my plan is for the day. Existence concisely contained. That board is all that matters now. When I use the toilet across the room, I need the disability handrail to ease myself down. The bathroom is a beige cube that reminds me of toilets on school camps.

A middle-aged orderly with liquid green eyes, long hair, and skin the colour of a drained beetroot comes into my room pushing a bed. Multiple gold chains on his neck hang outside his hospital smock. His name's Darren. He says he's here to take me to surgery. We chat. And he says he likes working weekends cos they're quieter, which I don't understand, then he explains that the trauma ward empties out on weekends, chills out, cos all the potential patients are out there getting hurt or about to get hurt and will arrive via ambulance or whatever on Monday. He says the routine keeps him stable, which is comforting to hear. He wheels me out of the room and into the corridor. From underneath Darren's jaw, I feel protected.

Quick bursts of movement in the corridors. Everyone coming and going, cutting in out and across, from room to room, the hive is buzzing. Old mates in wheelchairs, drugged faces and drugged bodies, undrugged soon-to-be-drugged everything. Blistered hands of long-term nurses access blister packs with blistering speed. Cupped impatient hands rise to dry mouths to swill water from a tiny plastic cup. A sad-looking guy in his thirties whose legs are so thin he could be snapped up and used for kindling sits on the floor. We miss him by millimetres. We pass a room where a big lady with no hair is being turned on her side by two female nurses.

Darren is a skilled driver. The hospital bed needs delicate handling. He wheels me out of the corridor towards the industrial-sized lifts. En route to the lifts, I'm wheeled through an area that's not grey metallic blue. It's lime green. A waiting area for friends and relatives of the traumatised. People in the waiting room are in various forms of uncomfortable-looking sprawl. Cheap lounge chairs pushed together to make beds. Jackets for blankets. Jumpers for pillows. The TV in the top right-hand corner is on. Dr Phil is saving a soul. The lifts come and there's another bed in the lift when we drive on. The old man in the bed looks like a fossilised bird in a nightgown. Shallow breath fogging up the oxygen mask. On the wall in the lift is an ad campaign for what will happen if you abuse prescription drugs. The photo is of a woman in pain with a massive capsule jammed on her head like her brain is one big pill.

Darren wheels me into the pre-op room. This surgery, one of four, is to use dissolvable stitches to fix my broken jaw. I'm now in the hands of the anaesthetist. This is the best part. Limbo between one world and another with a gregarious chap whose job is to ease me warmly into danger, albeit very low-risk. I'm in a pod about to be shot into space. Being prepped for my time travel. The anaesthetist is getting all the gadgets ready and the tubes and the swabs, while telling me about a movie he's just seen, and I can't remember which one, and I'm having a great time. If I could do this instead of going out on weekends, but then again, I'd be doing this one way or another. Going out. Staying in. There's no escape from the capsule. The last thing I see is the inside of the brightly lit dome planet and the main alien telling me to count back from ten.

* * *

I wake in the middle of the night to a helicopter rattling the windows and shaking the bed and I think I'm still adrift in the darkness of my mind. I've been asleep and unable to administer my morphine and wake in a lot of pain. Bits of jaw stitch jut out from my teeth like food scraps. The helicopter's movements throb it more. I press my morphine button multiple times till I'm no longer able to get more. There's chaos in the corridor outside my room, right next to my bed, but I don't really notice. It feels as though I've been cling wrapped then placed on a shelf in a quiet corner of a translucent fridge. I drift off.

(II)

I'm 15 and wake up in ICU. I'm here cos I arrived at the Children's Hospital via ambulance at the severe end of an asthma attack. By this age I'm already familiar with hospital, but it's my first time in ICU, and I'm scared. The kids here are so sick. It feels like I'm dying just being around them. I hate the grey rooms and the spectral vibe. I hate the smells. Shit and pine-o-cleen. Mothballs and piss. I gag every time I go to the toilet. I wake up in the middle of the night and there's a child shuffling past in a white gown. A tiny dead kid going for a walk. It frightens the shit out of me. I think I'm so spooked cos I've recently seen *The Sixth Sense* and feel like those kids in the film are all in ICU with me. Even to this day, twenty years later, that film terrifies me. When I get out of hospital, I swear to myself that I'll never go back.

(III)

At age seventeen, I brought my hurricane with me everywhere I went. Full immersion in all things hectic. But I had to yank back the reins cos something odd started happening to my body. Shooting pains and pins and needles began to ping up and down my legs. Soon, my feet and my bum were going numb, and I could only walk for ten metres, then I'd have to sit down. I had my seventeenth birthday, and it felt like I had skipped right to my seventieth. How time flies. I was diagnosed with spondylolisthesis. A condition which occurs when one vertebra slides over the bone below it, squeezing the nerves in the lower back, which then causes the pains and the numbness in the legs and feet and bum. And in my case, the inability to walk. It occurs in teenagers who do weightlifting or adults who've put some serious wear and tear on their back. I didn't lift weights and wasn't an adult. I was just getting amongst it. It turned out that I had severe nerve damage and had to have surgery.

They put four titanium screws in my lower back with a metal plate to secure the vertebrae. After surgery, a nurse had to help me walk. When I left the hospital, I had to wear a back brace, which was like wearing a cage around my upper body. It had clips in the front. I had to wear it every day for three months. I was strictly advised to not do any exercise or vigorous activities. I was seventeen! I was going to parties and socialising like any teenager would do. I'm not sure how many kids were wearing back braces to parties. To get around the awkwardness, I used to take off the back brace and stash it, usually in a bush, before going into the party. Then I would get it later. This worked. I just had to remember not to do the limbo.

(IV)
I'm 25 years old. I wake up at 2 am, dizzy, faint and sweating in my tiny room in my congested share house. Vision blurry. I sit up in bed and look at the dark square of moonlit sky above the top of the fence. There are hospital rooms with more space than my tiny box of a room. Although it does have a nice big window that I keep up with a stick wedged vertically in the sill. It's hot. But there's extra heat to my sweat. I'm lying in a damp spot – not piss, deep sweat. This is bad. I'm semi-hallucinating. This is like some tropical fever. I get dressed in shorts and a T-shirt and stumble out of the house and into the car. I drive myself to emergency at the Royal Melbourne Hospital. I manage to park the car nearby. The sliding doors whoosh open.

The fluorescents hit me as I walk through the door. The smell. I walk past the lime-green furniture and the rank-smelling security guard booth. Hectic BO trapped in a box. Stressed men. Stressed women. Hovering nearby is an old guy covered in grime with a puffed-out face. He's singing, stumbling in the general direction of everything. Operatic with eyes closed he rocks back and forth like he's on a boat in choppy seas. He goes silent, rocks some more and lunges for hand sanitiser on the counter like it's his last chance to be clean. Presses the plastic valve, gets the goo, and starts lathering his face, which he does while singing. In front of me in the line is an old Italian couple. The man has a beanie on even though it's 35 °C outside. And every minute or so the old man hacks up some phlegm, and the old woman catches it in a tissue-net poised at his bottom lip. A young blond brat who got injured playing tennis has his arm in his mum's blue sweater.

I stand in line behind singing old mate, who by now, has been spoken to by the BO taskforce. They come out in a cloud of stench to placate the man, who refuses to be placated. I'm shaking and faint and he's holding us all up, so I get his attention and ask why he's here. He squints at me, rocks a bit then comes close and gurgles that he just wants a medical certificate to show the police where he was. He just needs a piece of paper. Eventually, the nurses help him, and he gets his paper and staggers out. I'm standing behind the wire grille. The nurse asks the questions and when my temperature comes through the machine, she elevates her tone and tells me to sit down right away, and a doctor will see me soon. Do you have insurance? I do. I get called in. I get an X-ray. A doctor reviews my chest X-ray. I have pneumonia. Pneumonia. That's a first. Doc tells me I need to be admitted.

It's 6 am by the time I get to my allocated bed in a ward. My roommate for this stay is a guy in his 40s. I'm being wheeled in past him on the trolley bed. He looks at me, doesn't smile, then looks back at his TV. I find out he's here cos he fell off a ladder and cracked his skull open; I know this as my nurse tells me. She also tells me he's aggressive and to not bother him. I'm transferred into my bed next to a big window on the eighth floor. Out of the window the sun is halfway up the blue sky. I look at my roommate with the cracked head and the early morning news on. But I'm so zonked I go to sleep immediately, and sleep for nearly fifteen hours.

I wake up when a team of specialists led by a thin bespectacled man wearing a tweed jacket says my name. The thin man tells me that I will be able to go home later this afternoon as I've responded very well to the antibiotics. I should be fine in a day or two, he says, as long as I keep taking the oral steroid and the antibiotics. It's a brief stint, too brief maybe. I've got pneumonia. But if the wise man says I'm ok to go, then I'm ok to go. Later that arvo I get my medications, get dressed and I slip past my snoring roommate.

When I hit the corridor, I put my metallic grey jacket back on as though I never took it off. The same faces pass me on the way out. We pass each other in the corridor. We pass each other in our dreams. I go out through the lobby/reception area and stop to get a coffee at a Zagame's café complex. A monopoly on hospital cafeterias. A monopoly on suffering. People in pain need more coffee and cake. People whose loved ones are in pain need an extra pep-up. I order my flat white and take my ticket and look up at the screen and wait for my number. I get my coffee and go outside, past wheelchair lifestyles clouded in smoke.

(V)
I'm in a crack den. I'm in my 30s. This crack den is much like the crack dens of my future. My past. I'm waiting in my own internal emergency department with Nicholas Cage in *Bringing Out the Dead* ranting and raving at everyone. The blinds in the room are drawn, but a bit of grey, soon-to-be-hot summer light slips in. My buggy eyes are bugging out of my head. Sweating. It's summer, but the sweat is chemical. Dry mouth. I reach out and take the glass pipe from a mate's hand. Our speech is like our brains are being hit with one of those reflex-inducing hammers every second but instead of tapping knees the hammer taps our dopamine like a woodpecker. There's no end to anything. No beginning. My brain is bending like a palm tree in a cyclone in a stagnant room. I look across the room at Mat, who's drawing.

Something is happening to my chest; my breath is getting shallow, gaspy, but I can't tell if it really is or not. I test it by talking.

'Oi Mat, Mat, I'm testing my voice. Testing testing one two three.'

Mat's head snaps up like a kelpie who's seen another kelpie. It looks like his eyeballs are sweating. He responds.

'Three two one, live and clear Mr Magoo. Oi, look at this drawing.'

Mat holds up the page. Implacable feelings lurching thoughts bursting on to highways of paranoid traffic. He's drawn a cartoon crab wearing gold glitter pants and pointing disco-style to the sky. In the speech bubble he's written The Crab with the Golden Claws. It's funny but is it about me?

'Yo Mat, I can't breathe.'

'Huh?'

'I can't breathe.'

'Just take a few deep breaths. Relax.'

I try to, but I can't. I actually can't breathe.

'I gotta call an ambulance.'

'What?

'I'm freakin out man.'

'Just breathe.'

'It's not working.'

'Ok but I'll hide when they come.'

I call triple zero. I'm hating myself for so many reasons as I'm dialling. I haven't had to interact with ambulances for years. The voice says police, fire, or ambulance? I say ambulance. I tell the voice what's happening. The voice says they'll be there soon. Mat goes into a panic. He moves like a highly agitated goat. He throws things in the air, grabs a hat, puts it on his head, shakes his head, throws the hat away, pulls on some gardening gloves even though it's the middle of summer, gives me a hug, and runs out of the room. I hear the ambos pull up. I get up and go to the front door and open it. A warm-smiling man in a blue jumpsuit with red hair and freckles shakes my hand and says his name is Adam and his partner Bianca, who looks like a girl who comes first in many track and field events, takes me to the back of the van. It's air-conditioned, which is nice. I look around at the gadgets and the shelves of tubes and medical apparatus looming over me. I just want to breathe. As soon as the stethoscope hits my chest, as soon as safe hands start to move on the surface, I feel my chest expand, my breath comes back, and I exhale with such force that I feel like I'll turn into a tiny droplet of air. They tell me I just had a panic attack. After a minute or two my breathing returns to normal. I'm allowed to go. They tell me to take care and to stay away from drugs.

(VI)

I was back in hospital a year or so later for respiratory-related illness. When I got out again, I diligently waited a week to finish off my medications before I contacted Mat, who lives in a flat not too far away. I remember leaving my house in the early hours of the morning, my body doing weird things. Guts rumbling, butterflying, I stopped to gag and spit.

(VII)

I'm on the raft in the middle of the ocean and my Nautica sail is getting some nice wind behind it. I sip some water from the hat that I left out to catch tropical rain from the night before. Out here, it's just me, bobbing along under a flat blue sky. Day becomes night, and night becomes cold. I put my hat back on to get warm. A familiar shape rises in front of my raft. Searchlights crisscross my face. Scrubs. Fluorescents. A symphony of machines. I'm home.

5
Kids in a Kodak Moment
City Clubs & The End of an Era

BUBBLE

It's 3 am sometime in 2003 and I'm sitting diagonally opposite the entrance to Bubble nightclub, on a little step, smoking a ciggy. Bubble is on Francis Street, a 100-metre-long street off King Street in the CBD. It's basically just a few cafes serving tradies on one side, and a stretch of brick buildings with a couple of closed garage doors on the other. Little Chris is sitting on the step next to me and he's annoyed cos the fake ID I bought online from Thailand usually works, but it got spotted. I'm 17 but could pass for 15. If I'd wanted to be a jockey, I would've been the perfect height. Lil Chris barely gets asked for ID; he's tall and looks older than he is. My fake self, Steven McPherson, 19, goes back into my wallet for another time.

At Bubble the music is always hectic. Hard trance, psytrance and the heavy thump of hardstyle techno. Relentless high-energy tunes. Around this time a style of dance started to appear in city clubs like Bubble. A group of three rave kids would form a loose triangle on the dancefloor then launch into some kind of aggressive chicken leg thing, where each shuffle of the foot overlapped the previous shuffle in a barely visible shift, as though the multitude of movements was just one constant buzz. A sped-up Nutbush. And while they did that with their feet, they rolled their caps backwards over their heads like slinkies over their skulls. Occasionally, the leader at the point of the triangle would throw their cap in the air, shuffle in a 360, and catch the hat. The dance became known as the Melbourne Shuffle.

Out the front of the club, the queue is dominated by skinny fairy raver chicks, their boyfriends wearing big baggy jeans with blond tips in their hair. Bootcut jeans, slick, McDonalds arch fringes. Their pills and GHB already kicking in, they fidget, dancing on the spot, ready to burst. Glitter and rainbow-coloured wrist bands, fluffy pink leg warmers, skanky ski boots.

Before I realise how high I am, it's become immensely important that I listen to some club kid sitting on the footpath close by, ranting. The pills I'm on are strong. Brown As and Vs made famous by Andrew 'Benji' Veniamin, Carl Williams' no.1 hitter during Melbourne's Gangland War. 2003 was the most violent of all, with ten murders carried out in public places. This pill pressing was a gesture of supremacy over the drug trade. Initials monogrammed like cufflinks, to be worn with the suit of the city. It didn't last. Veniamin would be dead in a year. Carl out of action soon after. The pills were the talk of the town. Are the talk of the town. I'm on them now, so is Lil Chris, and so are a lot of the others I reckon. As we wait, they kick in.

Lil Chris goes in to get a stamp for me. When he comes out, we'll press our wrists together on a fresh stamp, clamp style, to transfer the ink to the non-stamped flesh. It's a good test of loyalty to see how long it takes for a mate to come out with a stamp. How long has it been, what's the time? Ah, there he is! Lil Chris is loyal. We walk around the corner. He dabs a bit of saliva (of which there isn't much) to the stamp to keep it wet, then we clamp. Tonight, it works. It often doesn't. We bounce back towards the entrance. I turn my reversible jacket inside-out and put on a cap. He tells me hang back five minutes then come in. I look down and hold out my wrist, no worries.

Inside it's nice chaos throbbing heads and potentially genuine threats in dark corners. Vietnamese gangsters of the real and wannabe variety, wearing singlets, Nike Air Max, slick trackies, glaring through laser beams. Hazy maze. Gaze n glaze. The sticky dance floor with babes shuffling and ruffling their greasy boyfriends' hair. I never really dance. When I'm all 'loved up' I just pinball more leisurely. Drugs streamlining my aggression. I stand at the edge of the dancefloor, boppin, and there's a babe cutting it up, mad sexy energy. But I feel eyes on me. I turn and some slimy fuck is staring at me, then staring at the girl like what're you lookin at, must be her boyfriend. He's squat and ugly, a toad in a jacket, so when I give him the finger it makes sense that he jumps into action off his meth lily pad. We shove each other, bravado for real, bravado for show, see how it plays on the edge of the dance floor. I look round for Lil Chris, and sure enough, he's right there. Bursts through the dancers, shoves the toad backwards. But he has mates, so we square off in the shadows. Then we back up and burst out of the club, merging with street crackle. Side by side, eyes rolling in our heads, silly and hectic, at the end of the city, just a couple of kids in a kodak moment.

DALLAS

Dallas Bar is no longer around. Before it was closed in 2013 it was one of the scummiest strip clubs on King Street. A place where young heads got excited, all geed up and ready to splash a few $20s here and there like it's the highest point of life. Tonight, I'm with Lil Chris. Back then, we were thick as thieves. We're waiting in the queue to get into Dallas. He brought a mate with him, name's Liam. He's chill. My ID works this time.

Dallas Bar is a two-tier box that emerged from a swamp and got fitted out for sleaze and crime. It was an unofficial clubhouse for the Hells Angels, until the cops got so much pressure put on them that they had to close. When we get in, it's compressed chaos, dancefloor in the middle, bar to the right, strippers upstairs. As soon as I'm inside all I want to do is leave, but Lil Chris gestures to the bar and lines up. Liam and I wait off to the side and size up the crowd, real from fake, threat from non-threat. We get plastic pots and go upstairs. Up here, it's less compressed. More room to move around. I was never a fan of strip clubs.

Two intimidating strippers in their 40s are doing their thing on stage, high-functioning junkies with high ponytails pulled back tight. Up here, desire represents itself in various poses. Boys are long or boxy with flat caps, baggy jeans and bum fluff, next to shirts worn long and out over black suit pants, spiky gelled hair and a lot of those pointed shoes that look like there's a matchbox jammed in at the end. They circle the black glossy stage where the two strippers bound and jiggle. The red interior sparkles in the metallic squares of the disco ball. They're putting in work, up and down the poles to the shake of a lower end note. This place is for the cheapskates, and fair enough, cos if you're one of those boys who go all the time, it hits the hip pocket. Dallas is the cheapest option, which isn't really that cheap at all.

We find a spot at the back with a slimy table and a couple of chairs. We sit. We sip our beers. We stare at the stage, but you can't sip and stare for too long. A strange-looking crook with a massive upper body and skinny legs like a praying mantis comes over. Heavy gold chains swing like a metronome when he moves. He leans in, metronome swings, asks us to buy more drinks, metronome swings more, pay for a dance or fuck off, metronome swinging like it'll catch some ear, but he stands up and steadies it, stops it. Liam, the pressure on, goes over and selects a stripper from the stage for a private dance. She winks, drop tucks her heels under her booty and sits down, flirt and haggle. Liam returns beaming, Lil Chris slaps him on the head all jovial and shit. She comes over to our table to grab Liam for his dance.

'Hi boyz, I'm Maryanne.'

Her soap opera porn voice soothes and stirs. Her high-class-smelling perfume transforms her into a low-class fantasy. The kinda fantasy you'd book a suite at Crown Towers and get on the gear with. I try not to stare too much, but she wants us to stare too much. She grabs him by the hand.

'Ok, it's time for me to shine Liam. Let's go.'

Liam stumbles as he gets up. Maryanne walks away towards a curtain behind the stage. Her aged ass cheeks jiggle. She's old enough to be our mum. Her pink g-string disappears further up her crack. Liam gives us the thumbs up as the curtain closes.

Most of the time Lil Chris looks like he's about to punch someone in the head. He carries himself like he could be a cop. Could be a crook. Keep em guessing. We sip our flat beers, making them last. No real plan for the night. Just let it unfold. Two new strippers are up on the stage and it's like they've come straight off a five-day bender with a power nap. The druggy energy, the chaos, the infusion of cheap drinks and cheap entertainment. Absorb it all. Extreme, high-stimuli saturation of the senses. Kick back in the eye of the storm and try not to get wet.

Liam pulls back the curtain with a smile that gets bigger with every step. Yeah, the boys the boys, gets recognition from a few pointy-haired brethren and gelled scalps nod and jostle. Lil Chris grabs him round the neck and pulls him in for a hug, then releases him. I speak first.

'Maryanne aye. From the look of that smile, she was as good as advertised.'

Liam with his gentle demeanour:

'Ha, definitely was Dom.'

Lil Chris laughs. I laugh natural too. The mood softens and we share a warm moment. A moment of relief squeezed between the levels of elevated tension. It's 1 am. We've got some whippa, but the toilets in this joint are too suss and too gross. Liam's car is parked at 24-hour parking up on Bourke and Russell streets, which is a bit of a walk, but I like knowing more chaos awaits when I get high. On the way out I see Maryanne sipping a drink at the end of the bar. Liam yells out and Lil Chris and I wave. She winks, then waves back. We head out into the swamp.

THE PALACE

I'd been in the club queue out front of Metro a few minutes ago but had to take a hike cos my ID got spotted. The security guard who spotted it was a mumma's boy in combat boots. And he held on to it, refused to return it. He told me to stay there while he spoke into the sleeve of jacket, a finger to his ear, in case a motorcade appeared. I slipped away and ran across the footpath. That ID was past its prime anyway.

I still have to get in though. To whet my whistle, I beep into the 7-Eleven across the road to buy a water. I beep out. It's a hot night in February and I'm wearing a sky-blue Ralph Lauren polo shirt with yellow insignia freshly racked for the occasion.

I sip my cold water outside the Hard Rock Café next to 7-Eleven at the top of Bourke Street and absorb the night. The Palace was a four-story club that hosted big druggy raves in the late 90s and early oughts. An elegant and grimy mix. Marble staircases and deep balconies. A time when crystal meth was exotic and kids from the suburbs drove to the city and parked at 24-hour carparks like it was a holiday destination.

There's an alleyway next to the club where crews of raggedy kids are bouncing around in the dark with dozens of glow sticks causing all the low-flying planes to crash. And that's where I go. I step off the gutter, then immediately step back on, moving out the way of a taxi that's been commandeered by a hen's night crowd wearing blow-up plastic penis balloons on their heads. They yelp for joy and jump in the cab. I make it across the road unscathed and into the alley where the kids, who are around my age and bit older, are frenetic. I catch glances. Hungry eyeballs, sweaty bodies. Heads from Melbourne's Southern Suburbs, city of Greater Dandenong, City of Casey, out west in Brimbank, Melton and some inner Maribyrnong suburbs in the mix. Moving past, I try the only side door, locked. At the end of the alley right next to the club is a set of stairs, with only five of the steps accessible. The rest are covered with a cage. The only way to get around it is if I invest in acrobatics.

To get to the stairwell beyond the caged-off section, I climb the tiny metal holes and it's difficult to get traction. I can only use three fingers on each hand and the tippy toe of each shoe. I make it to the top, and coil as best as a 5ft-6 man-child climbing a cage can coil, then spring out and over the concrete below, mid-air for a half second, clunk the bottom of the uncaged stairs above, swing there for a bit, catch my breath, then pull myself up over the railing. I climb up the back of the building that sits on top of the alley. There's a glass skylight in front of me and a wooden beam the width of a foot, going over a black hole. I get the feeling of being in deep water at a swimming spot and there's an amphibious creature moving upwards towards me. I run across the beam.

Now I'm at the front of the lower building, snug next to Metro like it's my buddy ol pal. I look out on to the street from my hidden spot. It's around 11 pm on a Saturday night and the city is pumping. That neon zip and clip, the drag of light in the wake of movement like cylinders of eternal childhood. Streams of emotion that I throw my line into and reel in all kinds of memories. Nobody looks in my direction. But if they were on the other side of Bourke Street outside the Hard Rock Café and looked across the road at the rooftop, they might see a little guy in a fresh polo shirt leaping from one building to another.

Now I'm on the roof of the Metro proper after jumping up and across. I'm really enjoying climbing and burrowing, trying to fuse my body and mind to the surface of the city, like there's no separation. It's hard to look like a roof, but I try. The roof rises then slopes down. I rise and slope too. It's at the bottom of the slope that I see the skylight over in a corner. I walk over, try to open it; it yields, lifting right off like a fun-size bottle cap. It takes a few seconds for my eyes to adjust, and when they do, I get excited.

Inside the bottleneck skylight is a huge attic. I climb in and perch on the beams like a pigeon, looking down at all the stuff. All sorts of nightclub clutter sprawled everywhere. I ease myself to the floor. Old furniture, rolled-up posters, sections of a bar, and boxes and boxes of shit. I'm about to go deep rummage-style in the boxes, but when I walk to the other side of the attic, I see steps going down to a door. I can hear the deep bass techno rumbling through the walls. This door may or may not take me into the club.

The door, painted a thick matte black, is down a flight of stairs. The walls on either side are also black. Going down towards it is like entering a black box. It's not like I'll open the door and it will swing out over the abyss like in that movie *Dark City*, is it? I hear a bird's wings beating somewhere. Wind coming in through the hole in the roof. All right motherfuckers, this is it. It literally opens right on to one of the dancefloors in the four-storey club. I act natural and move through the bodies. The deep techno darkness illuminated by iridescent faces, angles, and undulation. Kinetic beauty.

I don't spot the security guard coming towards me. He must've been told about someone on the roof, or he just happened to be right there. The impact. He tackles me to the ground, but I got muscle memory from U16s in the midfield, and as his tackle slips over my head, I get up and shove him hard when he's off-balance, sending him careening into a bunch of ravers. As he's getting shoved around, I make a move outta there, bumping and spinning through the blasting fragments of everything, all at once.

I walk quickly out the front. I see the supremo meathead mumma's boy in the combat boots who took my ID. I yell out to him. When he sees me, it's like someone shoved a hot poker up his bum. I shrug my shoulders at him, like fancy seeing you here. The gold and glass art deco doors separate the two streams of traffic moving over the marble floors, with two staircases winding left and right, and he can't get to me. I hold up a one-moment-please finger, I press my ear, speak into my sleeve, nod like I get the message, look up confirming the message, and give him the middle finger. He charges through the crowd after me, but I'm away. Buoyant with my Metro breach success, I cruise along the city streets. Happy as Larry.

KRYAL CASTLE

I thought Kryal Castle was a real castle but when I ask in all seriousness if there is a moat, my older brother, with his plastic rave bangles up and down his wrist like credentials turns around from the front of the navy-blue ford Fairlane, self-righteously delivers the info.

'It's a replica castle, built in the 1970s. No moat.'

I double down.

'By whom?'

Our driver, Emily, a pale girl who dyes her hair pitch-black and loves hard drugs, adjusts the volume on some psytrance.

'Keith Ryal. Took the K outta Keith, stuck it next to Ryal, and built a castle.'

It's funny. The carload, which includes two of Pad's fringe friends in the back seat who I don't really know, enjoy a decent cackle. They're decked out in mid-2000s rave style, black fat pants, coloured singlets. It's tacky, but whatever. I grab a CD case off the floor, Original Pirate Material I think, and set up a few lines, bump, then pass the others across the backseat. It's 2004 and at 18–19, I feel old, like my body and mind need to rest.

Out the car window, the sun is almost gone on a Saturday arvo in mid-December. The inner west becomes the outer western suburbs quickly on Ballarat Road. On the way to the turn-off for the Western Highway we pass through Ravenhall, where the main attractions are a massive Bunnings, a maximum-security remand centre and a medium-security prison. In 2013, Arnold Schwarzenegger will visit the 24-hour gym in Ravenhall and after a much-publicised workout, will be given the keys to the City of Melton by the mayor, a set of skeleton keys I reckon. We hit the Western Highway. Emily says we'll be there in thirty minutes. Pad starts reading off a clunky white MacBook on his knees:

'The 11-hectare property, in Leigh Creek just outside of Ballarat, is billed as a medieval adventure park and resort, comprising a fantasy-based castle and theme park, with seventeen four-star accommodation suits, retail outlets and established educational programs.'

I sniff hard, shifting the amphetamine to the back of my throat to get the trickle.

'Established educational programs?'

Emily again:

'Jousting college, shit like that.'

It's near twilight when we arrive, edging slowly through a field full of parked cars. I look out at the dark forest in the distance that surrounds an extinct volcano, called Mt Warrenheip; it dwarfs the castle at the base of the hill. I lose myself for a moment and get hit with a realisation that we're creeping towards the edge of a cliff, internal, external, conscious of something stored away that's been glad wrapped for a last hurrah. The rave scene, which my rave purist brother was baptised in, and was on the way out back in the late 90s, is well and truly on its last legs. Then we turn away from the forest and go straight ahead, bumping over grass towards the castle wall. The heat of a late summer day shifting to a warm chemical night. We pass numerous cars with music pumping. In a car in the distance, the passengers inside look watery and yellow, their open mouths teethy and exuberant, wild fish in mini aquariums.

We find a spot not too far from the 10-metre-high concrete castle walls. I leave the car and say I'll catch them later. I set off to find Steve, a close friend. He responded to an earlier text about my last-minute decision and tells me where he's parked. I weave through the field towards the castle's entrance where the sounds of psytrance rumble over the ground, red and yellow pulsating light breaching the top. I see the car, no light on, empty, then his head appears. I do a cop knock on the window, making him jump; he laughs as I gesture for him to please lower it.

'Sir, you fit the description of a village idiot who's been roaming the fields around here with an illegal jousting stick.'

Steve smiles that big warm smile, bright brown eyes that'll eventually be ruined by methamphetamines and enormous grief.

'Well officer, it takes a village of idiots to raise a true idiot.'

I ruffle his curly black hair and get in the back of the Holden Commodore. He asks:

'Did you get a ticket or what?'

I look at the top left corner of the wall, where the ground rises a bit and it might be possible to jump over.

'Nah, I'm gonna try get over the wall.'

'Ah King Arthur, that's the way to do it.'

I have my own drugs, always amphetamines. I get out my baggy and set a few lines off a plate that Steve passes back. I have a couple, chop Steve out. Then he asks:

'Want K?'

I remember him telling me he had K, which I've only had a couple of times. My drug behaviour is always up, only going down to crash and K being a sideways headfuck means it's only gonna fuck with my physical equilibrium, which is fine.

'Yeah, I'm keen.'

The next scene is us trying to walk from the car, falling over like little ones who've just learnt how to walk. We stumble around for a few minutes and topple over a low wooden barricade and everything is warm and glowing. The good thing about K is its lifespan: short. And soon we get our legs back. I tell Steve that I'm gonna suss out the wall and that I'll call him when I'm in. To get inside the castle proper, you gotta walk over a drawbridge. No moat though.

I go to the corner of the wall where the hill rises enough so that if I get a running jump, I can reach the top of the wall. And I do just that, timing it so the security guards are looking the other way. A shadow against grass, up and over. The drop is deeper over the wall, but I'm pumping adrenaline. I land on soft grass and roll away.

Shit is wild inside and I walk and dance around the young crowd in rave styles and frenetic movements. Steve is the only person who'd reply to a text in the heat of battle. He's with Wayne and Ivan, old friends. They're sitting at the edge of a massive amphitheatre where all I can see is a fluorescent wave of druggy bodies spread out under the sky. Steve is nearby, chatting to a girl with platinum-blonde hair, thick black eyeliner and pink ski boots. The main difference with this scene, and what sets it apart, is that picking up isn't the main aim. But then again, every guy knows that MDMA and other rave drugs, amphetamines etc, make your dick shrink.

Wayne, eyes as blue as the Adriatic inside a giant head. A head that'll be up on Crimestoppers in due course. He spots me.

'Domma ya fuck.'

He shakes his head and grabs Ivan's shoulder, spins him round. Ivan grew up fast and is on the cusp of change. After tonight, I won't see him again for years. When I do, it'll be to score, and when I meet him, he'll prepare his works casually, mixing his meth in the end of a coke can and shooting up while reminiscing about times like these. Tonight, he's free. Wayne again nods at me.

'This cunt got over the wall.'

I ask:

'Anyone seen Keith?'

Ivan and Wayne perplexed for a sec, then Ivan taps in:

'Probably cuttin shapes in the maze with Joyce.'

When the local council officially bans raves at Kryal Castle in 2012, due to too many drug overdoses, Joyce Ryall, Keith's wife, is quoted in the paper saying she doesn't understand what all the fuss is about.

We talk nonsense for ages then branch off in our own directions, no need to explain why. I go looking for my brother, feeling good, maybe have a dance. Even though there's thousands of people here, I know where he'll be. I set off to find him. I move through crowds of fully immersed ravers, cliqued up, with their water bottles in one hand and glow sticks in the other, doing the Melbourne Shuffle. And even though I vibe off the energy, I've come to hate the dance. I hate their clothes. I hate how they do everything the same. They remind me of an ad for Red Bull. I look around at all the people and don't know a soul. I scoop a few lines out of my baggy and the drugs provide relief. I grab a wheelie bin, hustle it to the edge of the crowd, and stand on it, looking out over the dance floor. Sure enough, I see him. Barefoot, baggy jeans, with pink angel wings on his back. I watch him dance, so content, in his element, head down, feet buzzing, and I'm envious of his connection to the music, to something. I jump down off the bin prepped for joy and beeline towards him. He sees me and we get amongst it.

I must be having a good time cos I don't notice the red-orange sunrise come over the massive dance floor, until it's all around us. I legit feel fucking great. I put my arm around my brother, who I notice is missing one of his angel wings and has acquired one of those hats with a propeller on it. He looks up and I spin the propeller.

Everything is getting lighter. Parts of the castle I didn't see in the dark are now very visible. I see a swinging wooden sign for a Ye Old Bookshope not far away. A big billboard advertising a medieval museum with photos of white families with their heads in stocks. Jousting stick furniture. A weird feeling of being lost at a school excursion. Soon we're all thinking the same thing, cos thousands of rave insect antennae start to twitch and tingle into overdrive searching for escape. One day closer to a come-down, to what comes after. The sunrise sweeping the scene out like a giant broom.

Pad is looking around wide-eyed and sweaty, and we both nod, let's get the fuck outta here. We walk toward the gate. And when we're through, an image greets us, an image I've never forgotten, as I see dozens of cooked rave kids spread out through fields of long grass like wild elves, and the whole scene is a fucken fairy tale.

6
An Archaeological Find

It's 2 am in the city, and I'm near the corner of La Trobe and Russell streets, where diamante Greektown meets duck-hooked shopfronts in Chinatown. The Exford hotel bottle shop in the thick of it. Stalactites Greek Restaurant does wholesome dinners for families, then later on pumps out takeaways for late-night hunger. Right next to Stalactites is an alley. I turn right, go five paces, then dip under the neon sign, Adult Discounters 10 am – 4 am.

The stairwell is painted bright yellow and blood red, the handrail sky blue, 90s throwback palette. On the landing of the first flight of stairs is a life-size poster featuring an ancient Roman wearing a black G-string and leather mask; he's holding one of those gladiator weapons that's a scythe/axe/something. Props for VHS-era porn. A plastic container full of condoms and pocket-sized packets of lube spill over the side and lie scattered around the stairwell. At the sex shop on the first floor, I pay $10 at the long glass counter to the old white guy with soft eyes and a firebreak who mumbles something I don't catch. He gives me my ticket and scroggin-equivalent for the journey: 1 x condom, 1 x lube. I beep through the second sensor and make my way up the next flight of stairs to the lounge. As I get closer to the lounge proper, my chaotic sexual energy builds. I go in.

The door clunks closed. On the back of it, there's a large swipe of paint with an arrow and EXT and I imagine a worker being instructed by their boss to take a tin of white paint and draw exit signs in high-action areas, making sure they're big enough to be seen clearly in the dark. Inside, the smell is sharp and immediate, yet distant. Smashed pine cones create a thin veneer. I adjust.

Tonight, the lounge is a mix of youngish guys in their early 20s like me, some on drugs, some not, middle-aged drunk public servants with their shirts untucked, and much older men. Inside to my immediate left is a cubicle, and in it, a waist-high, dark red leather bench with the foam stuffing ripped out. I see old eyes peering out of the dark. I get scumbag central vibes and keep walking. I go past a shadow on a tiny bench and it's like I've disturbed a man in camouflage, cos he rustles, materialises into life, rising as I pass. I come to the main part of the lounge where there's a movie-size TV, a mirror to the right of it, and two couches against the walls. Big windows to the street have been covered in black tape. A couch to the left, a long bench up against the wall to the immediate right, and another couch further along. On the flat screen, a couple of lumberjacks are slamming into each other in a log cabin.

I sit briefly on the bench against the wall smack-bang in front of the TV, waiting on the sidelines like I'm about to run on to the ground. Next to me on the bench is an old guy wearing a too-small T-shirt that's stretched over his belly, pants down around his sandals. From my seat on the bench, you can see and hear the most. A full-length mirror next to the TV that captures new arrivals, who only have two options to manoeuvre their way into the porn lounge. Either going straight ahead or turning right through the narrow dog-leg tunnel that can't fit two sets of shoulders simultaneously, to then pop out on to the black-tiled hallway, with neat glory hole cubicles like old phone booths on a film set. At the end of the tiled hallway is the TV once more. But if lurking in the serious dark is your thing, you continue past the loungeroom doorway through plastic PVC milk bar–style flaps to a small black room, where you can have your sexual encounters in the pretty much pitch black.

I get up off the bench and go for a walk along the black-tiled hallway and sidestep a youngish drunk guy in a suit. He's got his hands down his pants. Behind him is a tall guy, anywhere between 40–60 years old, thin as a lamppost. Smooth hands. He reaches for me. I meet his eyes, but I can't really see them in the soft yellowy light. I keep moving. Behind the unreadable lamppost is a young guy, around my age, champing at the bit, wearing shorts and a T-shirt. Drug sweat on his arms, his shoulders. The whites of his eyes pop when he passes.

In front of a glory hole booth at the end of the hallway is a one-person bench up against an ad hoc message board, where requests are written in pen, pencil, thick black texta, anything that makes a visible mark. Phone numbers scratched into flimsy wood with a key, or something else. I sit down, get out my phone and use the light of the screen to illuminate the messages I can't see, maybe saving a number for later. Raw gestures excavated for a second, then forgotten. I hear the beeping sound announcing entry into the porn shop below, and instinctively, as though caught in the middle of memory retrieval, I quickly get up and move away.

I need release. I've done my rounds. The lamppost hasn't moved, so I glance at him and go into the nearest booth. I lock the door. I turn on the light, making sure my shoes won't stick to the floor. I turn the light off. I wait. The sound of sensible shoes on the tiles coming towards the booth. He enters the one next to mine. The lamppost leans down, knee joints settling on an unaccommodating floor. Within seconds, a mouth appears through the darkness like an angler fish to take the bait. I close my eyes and let go.

A collage of creeps scatter across my memory. And the reasons why crash into a fundamental flaw. I'm not even attracted to men. Never have been. When I was younger and I thought my confusion might just be a classic sexual identity thing, I'd try to let men kiss me and be intimate towards me, but I found it impossible. Full body rejection. Essentially, I'm a straight guy, but for the last decade, I've been going to gay sex lounges, gay saunas, gay beats. I didn't know what I was searching for when I found these places when I was young. But maybe finding the cruising lounge was an inevitability.

I was 16 the first time I saw the bright yellow building in the city. On the first floor there was a porn shop, and the next floor was roped off. Initially I thought it might be the office where I could steal money. I was a busy little thief at the time, in and around the city. From the doorway I could see the worker behind the counter. I waited for him to turn away. There was a motion sensor on the wall in front of the next flight of stairs. The worker turned, and when he did, I climbed up, out, and over the rope and the sensor. I continued upwards. I got to the top and arrived in a smallish lobby area. There was a TV, couch, water filter, and clustered around the water filter (not talking) was a group of men that seemed demographically at odds. I stopped there briefly. To my left was a window looking askance down to La Trobe Street. Later, I would find out that those men would sit in the semi-dark, watching daytime TV while having an instant coffee or a tea in a styrofoam cup, sitting around (the window was always open and a constant reminder of reality) while porn played in the next room, as though it was just another activity like going for a walk or getting some groceries. I didn't go in that day, but I returned soon after.

I finish up in the booth and turn the light back on. I see a hand grab hold of half the glory hole. I clean up quickly and make sure to leave before he does. Minimise, deceive, and outwit my own awareness of what I'm doing. I try to block it out as though it doesn't exist, while still experiencing all the physical and psychological arousal that comes with it. It enters me, but I deny its existence. With the light on, I leave as quickly as possible. I open the main door and head for the bathroom. At the very clean sink, I run the hot tap for ages and only add a little bit of cold, so I feel the heat. I scrub well. It's nearly 2 am. I should go home. I look at my face in the bathroom mirror. I look away. The less awareness the better. The only thing I know right now is that there's no chance of sleep. I see only one option. And I take it as though that's all there ever was. I go back in for round two.

When I go back in, I go through the dog leg into the hallway and I pass a couple of older guys who look sleazy rich, like they probably live in the city or close by and post midlife crisis they've found a way to blow all their accumulated wealth. I pass them. I go back to the main lounge to rest the legs. The porn is boring. The main bench backs on to one of two largish rooms opposite each other off the main entrance. They're 2 x 2 m with a lockable door, a mirror, and a bin for tissues. I hear the flic of a lighter. The flic, then about 30 seconds later, the exhale, long and satisfied. Someone's smoking drugs in there. It's not such a bad idea. I could see what the go is. I get up and walk past the room. The door's been left ajar. I gamble and open it. The drug lad with the wild eyes is in there. In the semi darkness the lighter flic illuminates his keenness, shorts and T-shirt, the glass pipe in one hand. He nods at me, introduces himself as Ray. I go in.

We don't need to talk much. There's no need. Ray taps a chunky rock from a baggy into the pipe, sets the glow underneath, puffs a few clouds then passes it to me. The gear he's got is strong. Our eyes suddenly more focused than studious kids over important exams. The smoke twirls, and the world gets sharper. I pass the immediate joy back to Ray. This rank room is our new planet and we claim it like a couple of abandoned astronauts. Ray hits cloud 9 on the pipe in the corner. I can't control it now, my brain hit with the need to talk nonsense.

'Rainforest Ray attacked a low-hanging bandicoot but that's fair enough, whatta ya say Ray.'

He looks at me and a smile breaks out. Ray puts the pipe down and is on the talk.

'Damn free-range bandicoot was a fiend with no respect.'

The dumb chatter of fried idiots in a drug box. The idea of anything sexual has been put on the backburner, cos meth brain at full speed is Lance Armstrong on the sprint. Time is impotent until the novelty wears off. And sure enough, it does. Shit talk becomes cringe talk. Repetition. Silence. I'm looking at Ray and he's looking at me. We're like a couple of sexless mutes. I hear the porn groans and the disgusting awareness rolls over me. I tell him:

'Oi, I'm gonna bounce man, cheers for the burn.'

He's finished the toke, sitting in the corner. I see his young, weathered head properly. A sad sparkle in his eyes flickering away like a distant star. The sweat, the shorts, the situation is acute and profound. I'm reflected in his eyes. Linked through a subterranean current that carries him along. I know the movement of that current. But I'm not current. Fuck the current. I leave the room. Back to the bathroom. Back at the sink, I wash my hands thoroughly, scrubbing hard till it hurts.

***

When I began my porn-obsessed odyssey there was no Grindr, no dating apps. There was no jargon, like M2M, or P&P and the newly empowered, coming-of-age-on-the-gender-politics- cusp-generation hadn't yet arrived. There were cinemas like the Dendy, a Club X (now closed) that showed straight porn on two separate screens, with mauve-coloured, floor-length curtains separating the action. It was upstairs at the end of a lane off Chinatown, snug next to a multistorey carpark. The first floor of the Dendy was peeps and internet booths. Second floor was a small porn shop where the strippers working the peeps took their break. Lipstick-stained menthol ends squished in ashtrays. The cinema on the third floor was usually packed with all sorts. Sometimes it looked like a bunch of middle-aged men from the suburbs had come in on a tour bus; other times, the crowd varied dramatically.

The other place I went to, apart from the lounge and the occasional straight porn sex cinema, was the Club X in Footscray (now closed), which had an aptly named R.A.M. Lounge upstairs, but the only animals butting heads up there, were... Anyway, after the Lounge, Club X in Footscray was where I would go. $10 got you a 12-hour pass, but I never stayed any longer than was necessary to get the job done. There was a legit spiral staircase that you had to climb to get to the porn lounge, all rickety metal that jiggled underfoot announcing your arrival. The castle of porn awaits. Upstairs were tiny boxes with just a bench and space for two. And less-tiny boxes with a bigger bench, a TV above the bench, and space for three or four.

* * *

After my session with Ray, it's nearly 4 am, closing time. I return from the bathroom and sit on the bench in the main room. It seems like everyone has left, although I can hear noises from behind the plastic PVC curtain. I can hear the flic of the lighter. The sun won't be too far away. I force myself to get up and leave. I stop to wash again. I risk a look at my face. Over the span of nearly ten years, I've been coming to places like this, the same results, the same shame. I bury it deep down. I splash water over my face and get rid of the night's sweat and grime. I edge down the stairwell, pausing in the doorway to the alleyway, before pulling my cap down low and turning out into the dregs of the night.

I don't know exactly when I stopped going to the Lounge, but I think it was around the time I found internet dating; to be specific, OKCupid. I didn't have a smartphone, so I'd use it on my laptop with the whole dating layout across my screen in large print. I immersed myself in women, loved it, and loved them, or tried to. I was learning.

I remember one day I was walking through Chinatown and passed the alley next to Stalactites. I looked and saw the flash of the yellow exterior, the unlit neon sign, and it occurred to me that I hadn't been there in ages. In that moment, crossing the alley, the rush of experience was strong, and my heart went out to it, to a place that safely accommodated so many oddballs, addicts, loners, fugitives of self. Why had I spent so much time in these joints, over so many years? For the décor, the drugs, and a stab at eternity? I didn't really know, and I guess it didn't really matter. I kept on walking.

7
Coming of Age in the Wild West

I would've been 11 years old when I handed the note to the Vietnamese milk bar owner, followed by my $6 in coins. The note read,

> Dear Shopkeeper,
>
> Hello,
>
> I cannot get down to the shop to buy my cigarettes as I've sprained my leg playing netball, so I've sent my son to buy them for me. Can I please get Super kings super mild. Thanks.
>
> Yours truly,
> Linda Gordon.

My mum's signature was too hard to copy so I used my dad's, but it didn't matter, cos it didn't work. I don't know why I picked netball. My mum never played it or had any interest in it. Maybe I thought it would add prestige or I assumed local netballers smoked them? But if it was prestige I was going for, Superkings were the opposite. Their claim to fame was their length. They were long and thin and burned so quick cos the tobacco was so cheap that it was like smoking a lit fuse. The Vietnamese man with the mysterious mole hair sprouting from his chin looked at me from across the glass counter. He knew me well. I was the same kid he saw almost every day on the way to school, when I'd get a bag of lollies. He shook his head, handed me back the note and my coins, and shooed me away. Duck was waiting outside the milk bar. We were on our way to school, and when he saw me come out empty-handed, he shoved me, his cowlick wisping off his head, annoying like a dibber dobber.

'See, told you it wouldn't work.'

I jumped up and planted his annoying cowlick back on his head then pointed at the front of the shop.

'Did you see the sign in the window, no cowlick dickheads near the shop!'

In ten years, Duck would become a pumped-up steroid-head who'd got in with the wrong crowd, be charged with accessory to murder, flip, turn Crown witness, and disappear. On this day, he was just an 11-year-old on the way to school like me. I gave up trying to shove him and we kept walking.

Duck and I started smoking when we were 10 years old. His nickname was Duck cos he had fat lips that squished, then pouted, like a duck, and he bum-sucked his ciggies and they came back wet. He didn't like smoking as much, which was lucky, cos I hated sharing with him. We smoked at Duck's place, an old weatherboard house, next to the oil refinery and the empty warehouse complex where we played. His old man didn't have any sense of smell, some kind of accident at work years ago, so he never smelt the smoke when we opened the window and smoked in Duck's room. Inside the front section of his house, it was a ramshackle hoarders' lounge room where his dad would sit in his big chair watching Foxtel. A small bathroom and Duck's room off the lounge room. Then there was a T-junction hallway that led to the back part of the house. At the end of the hallway, it opened up to chrome benchtops and high ceilings, and everything looked new. Outside some fancy French doors was Princess, an aggressive dingo cross that would run the length of its chain and buck whenever someone appeared. Duck's mum was a local councillor. Pale, stern, and bespectacled like a teacher. We avoided her at all costs, and we spent the least amount of time in the new section. One time Duck burnt his prized cowlick when I jacked up a lighter, and when his mum found out I was banned. That was ok though cos he wasn't the only one I smoked with.

I learnt to inhale from Yarraville West's coolest kid in 1995, Dave Maddox. He was two years older than me. We were in a back lane in Kingsville, next to the abandoned caravan, and I coughed so much that tears ran down my cheeks. In a few years, Dave would be a Footscray smackhead in a white Country Road jumper, bootcut jeans, Nike Air Max and a gelled fringe. By age 11 Roy, another local kid who loved smoking ciggies, was the size of an adult, with pimples and a breaking voice. He always wore his too-small faded green trackies and a too-small yellow T-shirt. He would've been constantly outgrowing his clothes. He smoked so much that he had yellowy-brown nicotine stains on his fingers.

The last time I smoked with Duck we'd wagged school, crossed over Anderson Street on the city side of the station, walked past the ugly maroon bus shelter, avoided Dad and Dave's dirty old shop next to the station as we always did, turned down Murray Street, crossed over Fehon Street, like we were on the way to school. As planned, Duck and I saw big Roy waiting near the alley where we smoked sometimes before school. Duck and I had brought a change of clothes, but Roy always wore the school uniform, which was optional. Roy had ciggies, a little packet of Holiday 20s, thin as toothpicks. He gave Duck and me ciggies. We both watched Duck's lips going to work on the butt, cowlick in full cowlick mode, as he soaked the shit out of the ciggy. We never smoked together again.

* * *

In the early 90s our family left the rental we could no longer afford in the inner south-eastern suburbs and moved to Yarraville. Or in Dad's case, back to Yarraville. Dad and Mum were late-season hippie slackers, a working-class lad and a middle-class journo, and now finally, totally broke. There was no place left to go but 28 Sussex Street. He'd left twenty years ago, he thought, for good. But Hazel his grandma died, just as we hit rock bottom. She'd been born in 28 Sussex Street, before World War One, and the place was slated for demolition. But somehow Dad got a loan to buy it, 88 grand, split between Hazel's four kids, and so in 1993, we moved in.

The front of the house was part of Sussex Street with a sharp divot turn in the middle, ours the only house on it, neighbours, and then friends, Rhett and Lynn a little further down. The back part of the house had a back gate that opened on to Wilson Street, a cul-de-sac behind the house. At the other end of Wilson Street was the train line. Ballarat Street, one of the main shopping strips, cut the streets in two.

Around the corner from our house on Ballarat Street was the Bluestone Hotel. A double-storey bluestone pub that we weren't allowed to go in cos it was considered to be too rough. My great uncle Michael was the SP bookie there in the 1950s–60s. It's now a Thai restaurant; they kept the façade and fitted out the inside, so it looks like a thousand other suburban Thai restaurants. Laneways that crossed the length of five parallel streets connecting close-knit homes, brick units, cladding bungalow joints – where neighbours on opposite sides of the lane could chat over their fences. The occasional concrete mansion where, of a Saturday morning, immaculately groomed Greeks in dressing gowns could be seen blasting errant grass off their driveways. There was a cake shop, a video shop, and a souvlaki place that I was scared to go in cos Peter would be there, and when he saw me or my brother, he'd put the small microphone to his neck, press a button and lip synch a frightening hello. Opposite was Con's Barbers, where I told Con I wanted to have a flat-top like Van Damme. Con said my hair was too fine, I insisted, he tried, it didn't work. I was devastated. Up a bit on the corner of Ballarat and Anderson streets is Railway Hotel, where I got called a poofter for wearing red pants. Turn left down Anderson Street towards the train line, past Marita's curiosity shop owned by the original Yarraville gentrifier, Marita. Manikins wearing berets, incense burning and a black cat I wanted to kick in the face.

Then a few doors down just before the train station is Ha's Tobacco, where you could get a kilo of damp chop chop in a shopping bag for $5.

There were two milk bars, the one I went to on the way to school, and the other one around the corner from our house, on Stephen Street, where Duck lived. It had way more selection – Fads, Big Boss Cigars, and they sold singles (individual ciggies for 50c). On the other side of Stephen Street was the Yarraville Club. A sprawling pensioner pokies place, live music like Grimmy Barnes and his Band, Johnno Jovi, local rip-offs. In a small bluestone house behind the Yarraville Club was where my friend Gary lived. Gary was tall and skinny with a big head, gap teeth, unlike his old man, who had a small and angry scorched sultana head. Across the road from Gary was where Jaydon lived in a small brick unit, in a block of units. His old man was a Scottish bus driver, only ever saw him in his uniform, and whenever I saw him in his house it was always dark. Sometimes I'd go see what was going on by the river, where enormous freighters would be coming and going, and there'd be old men fishing off corners of the jetty. In my mind, the fish they caught would be mutated and gross like the three-eyed fish in *The Simpsons*.

Because 28 Sussex Street had two entrances, we had two streets of friends. Out front we hung out with the tomboy Macedonian sisters, mostly Danni, who was 11, had a moustache and rode a BMX with pegs. Next to them were the Tongan boys. A few houses down in the other direction was the Brennan family. Mother Brennan was short and stocky with hard flat hair like a small frying pan. She walked high on the balls of her feet, urgently. Her daughter Amanda was a head taller than her, skinny as bamboo and also bobbed along. Her son Allen was my age and a reluctant bobber but was always pulled into line. The father, a quiet man who wore cardigans, didn't leave the house much. When the three main Brennans were on the move, they'd crest the concrete, eyes down, heads bobbing, seals in a pod. Out the back on Wilson Street were the Fijians. Owen was my age and good at sports; we became close friends quick. He had an older sister, Angela, who wore baggy Fila T-shirts, was always in trackies, dyed her hair, and had a waterbed.

Video Flash on Ballarat Street was like entering a VHS canyon, cliff-top shelves, with a clunky beeper at knee level that released a long, sad, cowboy 'bing bong' whenever someone entered. Scuffed-up old green carpet, weird movies, faded movie posters. There were human-sized cardboard cut-outs and the system was that whoever wrote their name on the back of the cardboard cut-out got to take it home. I had a 6ft cardboard cut-out in my room of Jackie Chan in *Rumble in the Bronx*. The big white counter, where you paid and handed over the empty video case for the tape from the back, was just high enough that I could see over it.

In 1996, the same year my footy team, North Melbourne, wins the Grand Final and I have my face painted in royal blue and horizontal stripes, I remember getting off the train with my family, and the unlit neon sun that sits on top of the abandoned cinema near the train station, is glowing in the night. Soon, a guy with a blond perm is driving around Yarraville in a canary-coloured convertible; the driver turns out to be the guy who purchased the Sun Theatre and re-opened it as a film society.

The last time a car failed to make the turn on Sussex Street, it barely clipped our fence. But it did plough right into Rhett and Lynn's living room. They moved out soon after. We never saw them again.

We went in 2001. Video Flash closed in 2006. It was replaced by a cupcake store. Which is now also gone.

* * *

Fiona, a tough local with purple-green hair and a raspy voice, is a teacher at Yarraville West Primary School, and between drags on her ciggy, she's trying to talk to some 11-year-olds about life in a newly created class at my school called PD or Professional Development. Primary school kids can't be expelled, but I was doing everything I could to challenge that. I'd been removed from class so often that something had to be done. So, alongside another teacher, Mary, who had a buzzcut, often wore cargo pants, and taught me in Grade 3, telling my parents that I was destined to be a bad kid, Carol enlisted Sharon, the school principal, another buzzcut, but with RM Williams and jeans, to come up with a solution. Carol, their spiritual leader, gets carte blanche to put her lived experience to use.

The class itself consisted of taking me and some other kids out of class for one hour every day and going for a walk, well, Carol's long loping strides meant it was more of her walking and me sort of jogging, while she puffed away on her ciggies, delivering words of wisdom. She wore black jeans and a black vest over an untucked white shirt, cowboy boots and lots of noisy bangles that clinked up and down her arms when she got serious. I can't remember what she said. The other kid in PD was Caleb, a bully that everyone was scared of. We became friends.

I also looked forward to the hour of PD cos we would inevitably walk past the class where my primary school girlfriend Kristina was. Blonde, half-Polish and popular with a double-barrel last name, we were the king and queen of the school for nearly two years, until she dumped me halfway through Grade 6, saying she had to move on. By then I was no longer going to Williamstown High with all my friends, after I'd been caught shoplifting at Harris Scarfe at Highpoint. My parents removed me and sent me to Simonds Catholic School. But I didn't really care, cos towards the end of Grade 6 I was having too much fun messing about, and I was spending lots of time with Caleb.

Caleb was a big spoilt kid with ghost-white cheeks who was always in flashy new sports gear. He had a deformity on his left hand: he literally had a toe for a finger. The story went that he'd lost a pinkie under a lawnmower when he was a kid, literally lawnmowed off, and his mum, a velour tracksuit bouffant with a nest of dyed red hair and gold hoop earrings, decided that Caleb might have a better life if he had the toe that most resembled a pinkie finger removed, and surgically attached to his hand. Could you take the little toe off a left foot, and turn that little toe into the pinkie finger on someone's right hand? You could. It looked like a translucent jelly baby or some kind of shark penis.

Caleb didn't have a dad, but he had Vincent, essentially a professional chaperone who barely spoke, just drove us everywhere. He looked like he'd come straight out of the army: clean-cut, in polo shirts and slacks, wore a gold watch. The family plus Vincent lived in a house in Taylors Lakes, an outer western suburb of Melbourne that hustled its way on to the map when a multi-million-dollar shopping complex called Watergardens was built there in 1998. When Caleb's mum wasn't attaching toes to hands, she was buying West Coast Coolers for me and Caleb. And when she found out I was stealing valuables from pool changerooms, she encouraged me to steal stuff for her. If I had it my way, I would've never wanted my mum to meet Caleb's mum.

In my mind, the difference between my home life and Caleb's life was never meant to be openly acknowledged; my family wasn't supposed to exist. By age 11, I was desperate to get away from all things Gordon. So when my mum came to pick me up in our battered Datsun 200B out the front of their house, I watched in horror as both mothers met for the first time. It was a brief encounter, but memorable. Caleb's mum, wearing black leggings, leopard print wedges, hair booffed, an electric-blue fluffy jacket with hood, and a face packed with makeup wiggled towards the car; meanwhile Mum got out wearing a light blue skirt and shirt, with sandals, no makeup. They shook hands and I cringed so bad. I was angry at my mum for being natural-looking. I sulked all the way home. Mum never knew about West Coast Coolers, or that we were allowed to watch whatever we wanted, and more importantly, that Caleb's mum encouraged me to steal.

Caleb and I set fires, but I wanted to do it by myself. My idea was to set multiple bins on fire at the same time on the same platform, at Flinders Street station at peak hour, in a sequence. At the time, the bins on train stations were tins drums in red rusted metal containers with a black bin bag, about belly button height for me. I was willing to get grotty to get the job done. So, at peak hour one day I walked casually on to platform 6 & 7, Frankston, Pakenham, and Cranbourne lines, leant into the bin, lighter in one hand, paper in the other, lit it down low, dropped it, then moved on to the next one. By the time I got to the end of the platform, I'd set three bins on fire, with varying success, depending on what was in the bin. Then I crossed to a few platforms over and waited, watching the reactions of people when they first saw smoke, their response.

One of the bins must've had some seriously combustible shit in it, cos while the flames of the other two barely flickered over the lip, the third bin was raging, flames crackled double the size of the bin. I heard sirens. The next bit was good too, again, the response, but this time of the firefighters who hustled to the platform in their bulky overalls and plastic hats, dragging a hose, hosing the bins down. Some nerd applauded them. Then they left. The bins drenched and gross. I got a real thrill out of watching the fire. When I left Yarraville West Primary, the technique of taking me away from my local friends and sending me to a school I'd never even heard of did have some effect; mostly it took me away from Caleb.

My parents told me not that long ago they were genuinely afraid of Caleb and were frightened something terrible would happen to me. My mum in particular mentioned an incident I recall. I was supposed go camping with Caleb, Vincent and his mum, but after driving out to the campground, for whatever reason, we just drove home again. All I remember about the drive was at one stage, there was such thick forest either side of the car that the daylight was blocked out. When we got home, I didn't call my parents to tell them that we were no longer going camping for the weekend and I can't remember what Caleb and I did. But when Mum found out we hadn't gone camping, and I hadn't called for three days to explain, and that neither Caleb's mum or Vincent had insisted I do, it struck her as not quite right. Caleb vanished; the last I heard he'd become involved in organised crime. Kristina works at Bi-Lo in Yarraville, has a young child and lives in the same house she grew up in, opposite the school.

I once saw Fiona at the Commercial Hotel opposite. It was opposite the docks in Yarraville. My dad took me and my brother there, where we'd have a red lemonade, eat crisps, and play pool. I could just reach over the table to shoot. There was often live music on in another room, a strange mix of older cover bands and fresh out of high school local indie bands. Once, I heard a raspy voice coming out of the faded door to the band room – *I loved the words you wrote to me, but that was bloody yesterday, I can't survive on what you send, every time you need a friend* – I opened the door, and through smoke, I saw Carol with a Maton acoustic guitar, a drink and a ciggie on a bar stool singing the stuff they sang then, 'Closer to Fine', 'Because the Night'. Of the ten or so people in the audience, I recognised only Mary and Sharon, both wearing lipstick, their respective buzzcuts spiked.

I wonder now whether she was happy cranking out inner-city hits in a stale pub on her day off, or whether the job was a fallback, and what she actually thought about what she did. The fact that I'm writing this now could be that maybe she did say something in the class, in Professional Development, something that meant nothing then, but over time had its effect. Whatever it was, it did fuck all for Caleb.

* * *

By the time Lindy and Terry Gordon brought their family to 28 Sussex Street Yarraville, they had explored all the possibilities the 70s could offer a boho couple. Lindy had been a waitress and a cinema usher, worked as a journo on a local paper, and done freelance work. Then, in the late 1980s Lindy began running a clothing shop that her mother Maria had owned. It was called Lorna Fashions and was in a shopping mall-style location in the outer suburbs. Lindy hated it. But it brought in enough money for our family; with my brother born in 1984 and me in 1986, things were ok. Then the recession hit in the early 90s and the shop went under. Dad picked up work wherever he could. And given he had no real qualifications, he got work cleaning toilets at St Vincent's Hospital, and washed dishes. Over the next few years, raising two young boys in a financially stressful environment was putting serious strain on their marriage. It wasn't always like that.

Lindy and Terry met at a party of a mutual friend. Terry, with his long hair and beard, suit jacket and cigarette, encountered Lindy, with her auburn-coloured hair in a tomboyish short fringe, a silk scarf wrapped around her neck, wearing a dress, overcoat, heels, smoking, drinking. Terry told Lindy that his favourite film director was Sam Peckinpah, who, at the time, was on every educated liberal's hit list, as *Straw Dogs* with its infamous rape scene had been released. Dad delighted in getting under the skin of the boho liberals. And Mum, being a boho liberal herself, tangled with Terry but secretly thought it was a courageous move to take such a stance when everyone else was against the director. And when she heard about his record collection, she wanted to see it.

Terry and Lindy were a pretty typical story of the time, a working-class lad and a hippie girl from the middle class getting together. Soon after, they moved in together in the mid-1970s, renting out a small miners' cottage in South Yarra. Went to the cinema, to parties, went out for a meal every now and then at a time when you could get a big steak at Florentino's for $7. They also travelled to London and Europe.

* * *

Lindy was the middle sister of three, sandwiched between Bronwyn the blonde and Cathy the baby, as Cathy was many years younger. Mum spent most of her childhood with a bowl cut, reading, swimming in their pool at Harkaway, and dealing with Maria, her mum, drinking so much that she had to be put to bed. When my mum wasn't on edge at home, she was waiting for her dad, Geoff, who was often away on business for months at a time. And when he was home, he was also a heavy drinker. As soon as she could Mum moved out, and then she was living with Bronwyn. Terry had to repeat Year 12, but nonetheless when he completed it, he was the first person from his side of the family to do so.

Before we moved to Sussex Street, we were living in Hughesdale, where there was a backyard big enough to play cricket. Dad's best friend at the time, Ahmet, a working-class Turkish guy who'd published a book of poetry back in the day, would come over and play cricket. Mum and Dad smoked inside, listened to records, and had a good time. Dad was a cool customer; he smoked, drank and knew about movies, and he was funny. Mum was likewise, but she loved to dance. And so did I. And when we were young kids, Dad would put on Johnny Johnson, and I would dance. Dad was always ironing, and therefore I thought that ironing was very interesting, especially the way the steam from the iron would fluff and flush the air when he did his shirts. Everyone smoked then. Everyone drank then.

Everyone loved Ahmet. He and Dad had been friends since they were in high school. Around 1990, Ahmet took off and moved to the south side of Chicago to start a newspaper. Bronwyn's first husband Tony, one of Ahmet's closest friends, had just died in a car crash, and before his death, he'd gotten a plane ticket to join Ahmet in Chicago, and now there was a spare ticket. In late summer of 1992, when I was six and my brother eight, Mum told us that she was going to Chicago, telling Dad that she was taking the ticket and he was to stay home and look after us kids. Lindy left Melbourne in late summer of 1992, and was gone for two weeks.

A year or so earlier, prior to Lindy taking off to America, there was a time when Dad wasn't living with us at all. Mum basically kicked him out as he wasn't contributing, and he went to stay in a friend's bungalow. In the meantime Mum claimed the single parent pension and Dad jumped back on the dole. Dad would visit us on the weekends, but he was no longer living at our house in Hughesdale. Terry knew he had to make something happen to try and save the marriage, as Lindy was drifting further and further away.

It was at this time, in late 1992, early 1993, that the house in Yarraville that Terry had forgotten about came up for sale. It was on the market for $88,000 and Dad managed to get a bank loan for the deposit. My brother and I aged 7 and 9 were none the wiser. To me it was an adventure, going from one side of the city to another on the train. And not just to go to Rose's house in Altona, where we often went, and always came back, across the city to Hughesdale.

Now we only lived a few train stations away. It was Dad's last-ditch move to save our family, and even though it wasn't the ideal destination – when Dad told the real estate agent we were moving to Yarraville, he asked, where's that? – it worked. We were all back together.

* * *

Rose O'Farrell was born at 28 Sussex Street in 1929, and lived there until the age of 20, when she was sent to St Joseph's Foundling Hospital in Broadmeadows, after becoming pregnant, although no one knew or talked about who the father was. At the age of 14 she had won an academic scholarship to St Columba's College in Essendon, a prestigious, all-girls Roman Catholic school. She was bright enough to have the latter part of her education paid for. But as the family could only afford to equip one child with uniform and books, they picked Michael, the oldest son. He was supposed to be going to South Melbourne Technical School to learn a trade, but never went, wagged school, and hung out with mates. So, instead of a potentially interesting career, Rose worked in the fields and kitchens for the St Joseph's nuns before a girl was born, adopted out, and Rose came home to 28 Sussex Street.

In 1952, still bitter at the unnecessary refusal of a higher education (a bitterness she never lost) Rose went to work at Dickies towels, in Hyde Street Yarraville. Dickies was a factory that wove cotton, imported from England, to make towels. By the time Rose came to work there, they were still using specifically trained workers, who would each place an individual thread around a giant bobbin situated at the end of each line, and once that foundational thread was done, it went off on its journey to the other end of the factory, where Rose and countless others like her would prepare and fold the finished product into boxes for distribution.

Dickies produced high-quality cotton towels, large striped beach towels, tea towels. The factory did well until the 60s and 70s, when it began to struggle with new tastes. So it took one of its underwear lines as its lead project and became Bonds in the late 1970s. The hard-chested Anglo figure of Chesty Bond grinned over Yarraville from the side of the factory until it closed in 1988 and the company became an outsourced brand.

Rose worked at the end of the line, where the trucks would come and pick up the boxes of towels. And by this time, she was eager and anxious to meet a good man. Rose came into contact with a dapper little delivery driver called Neville Gordon. Neville Gordon, a working-class boy from Melbourne, scrubbed up all right. Rose was very much in love with Neville. They were married in 1952. My dad, Terrence Neville Gordon, arrived in April 1953.

Terry was born with one eye missing and the top of his skull caved in. The divot ran from the upper forehead to the bottom of the eye socket. The obstetrician Les insisted on, as he came cheap, had told Rose that even though she was having excruciating pain, the baby wasn't ready to come out. The pain was my dad's head squished into her hip. He stayed in that position long enough to do the damage, losing his right eye. Before Les left the family, they lived in Box Hill. He opened a small fruit and veg store in Port Melbourne, but the shop didn't make enough money and soon went bust.

Les left the family five years later and moved to Queensland, where, before making money in real estate, he sold fluorescent lights door-to-door, and called himself Lee. He wouldn't see his son again till Terry was 17. Dad was struggling to finish high school, having failed his HSC, so Lee reached out and told him he'd pay his way and his tuition at a Christian Brothers school in Queensland. Dad went up there but never went to school. He went swimming instead. Dad got expelled after missing too much school. Lee got Dad work as a labourer, but he only lasted a day, just went back to the beach. Lee told Dad to piss off. So Dad went back to Melbourne, and finally finished high school. It would be nearly fifteen years till he saw Lee again. He came down to Melbourne for Mum and Dad's wedding in 1983. He gave them a George Foreman grill for a wedding present.

By the early 1960s it was Rose and Terry vs the rest. And throughout the 1960s they were on the move, a few places in quick succession, a longer stint living in a commission flat in South Kensington where Rose's then-boyfriend lived. Evan, as he was known, was from NZ, a World War II veteran, ex-jockey, alcoholic. He worked on the docks at Port Melbourne. He was a very little man with a temper, abusive towards Rose. And one day, Dad, who by then was 16 and already 6ft, got into a fight with him. Smithy got the worst of it, and he kicked them out. With nowhere else to go Rose and Terry returned to 28 Sussex Street. It was 1970.

Rose's father Jack died in 1971, not long after Rose moved back to Yarraville. Jack had worked most of his life at ICI Munitions factory in Braybrook. When Jack wasn't working, he was drinking at home. Rose's mother Nelly outlasted her husband by twenty-five years and died in 1993. Nelly raised five children at 28 Sussex Street and worked most of her life as a tea lady at a place called Eliza Tinsley's in the city, where she wheeled a cart stacked with urns of tea and coffee to employees. The façade of Eliza Tinsley's is still there on Spencer Street. A grand brick building with 'Eliza Tinsley' in big cream colours.

The eldest Slattery was my great-uncle Michael. He was part of a unit that was sent over to 'clean up' after they dropped the bomb in Nagasaki, and when he returned, he did what all traumatised men did in those days: drank himself to death. Yet before his death in his 40s, he worked in the wharves and was the local SP bookmaker in the area. The next Slattery was Yvonne, who married Percy Freeman aka Jackie Daniels the boxer and lived in Tottenham. Next was my great-uncle Patrick, a closeted gay man who smoked Craven A cork-tipped cigarettes and enjoyed spending Sunday afternoons in the fernery at 28 Sussex Street listening to an opera show called *Singers of Renown* on Radio National with his dark hair immaculately combed, wearing brown slacks and a light brown cardigan. Rose was next, and then the youngest Slattery, Walter. I never met Walter. He worked most of his life at the Newport railway yards, painting the railway cars, and when he wasn't doing that he listened to classical music, of which he had an encyclopaedic knowledge.

Rose didn't stay for long at 28 Sussex Street after their return in 1971 and got a second job to support Terry and herself. Her daytime gig during the 1970s and 80s, till it closed, was at Nugget Shoe Polish in Williamstown. Rose's job at Nugget was to pull a big lever that punched the small nugget of shoe polish into its canister. She did that all day, then at night was a barmaid at the Spotiswoode (now Spotswood) Hotel next to Spotswood train station. Filmmakers used that pub to film some of the scenes in the film *Spotswood*. Around 1972 Rose met Bruno when she was working behind the bar. She moved in with him in Altona.

Before our family moved to Yarraville, we visited Rose and Bruno in Altona often. Their weatherboard-cladding house was painted a bright fluoro lime colour and sat back on the block, with a wonky, waist-high brown fence with un-mowed grass that was never shorter than knee height. The front entrance was dark, the kitchen small, which was ok cos they didn't cook much anyway. The best part of their house in Altona was the sunroom just past the kitchen, which was Bruno's favourite place. He'd sit out there in his recliner in grey slacks, wearing a white singlet tucked into his slacks, hair brillcreamed back, a can of XXXX and he'd watch his beloved cockatiel Stupid (it was actually very smart) walk up and down on its perch, and he'd talk to the bird in his heavily German-accented English, while raising his beer:

'Ahh zeestupidd, hehe.'

The bird talked back with:

'Stupid stupid stupid.'

Bruno had a bad back, and when he wasn't sitting in his chair, he leant forward when he walked.

At that time we were living in Hughesdale and there was no indication that we'd live in the west, which in the early 90s seemed weird and exotic. By now Rose was in her 70s, slightly built with blonde-white hair, close cropped, bright blue eyes in a playful gaze. Out of the grey of the old western suburbs, she had come into her own. She wore pleated plants, white runners, plain-coloured jumpers with fluffy patterns, sometimes a jumper with a bird on it. In summer, blouse and slacks with lightweight sandals on her feet, sitting out the back at the Altona house at the red picnic table underneath the sun-bleached, yellow beach umbrella with white tassels around it. Rose was talkative, funny, liked a punt on the horses, and always had her VB nestled in a stubby holder.

Rose and Bruno moved to a country town called Elmore near Bendigo in the mid-2000s. Rose died only a few years after the move. Her sister Pat said it was the move itself that killed her, as Bruno couldn't lift anything due to his back and Rose literally had to move everything. Bruno had a shed full of tools, a whole room full of his war memorabilia, and countless jars of pickled onions. Bruno died five years after Rose. He was found dead in his motorised wheelchair that had tipped over in the backyard with a slab of beer still in his arms.

* * *

I'm in the living room looking at my brother's *MAD* magazine when Dad comes in. He's got a six-pack of Boags and a couple of videos in an open cardboard package from the Australian Centre for the Moving Image (ACMI), under his arm. He peels open a Boags 500 ml can, puts a cassette into the player, and soon there's intense stabbing music, followed by a black and white title, *The Asphalt Jungle*, expanding across the screen. Dad slumps back into the chair.

'Wanna watch?'

'Yeah!'

He has a few swigs of his beer then looks over at me sprawled on the floor close to the screen when I ask him:

'But what's an asphalt jungle?'

He nods outside.

'It's like the city.'

Mum's in the kitchen, and the whole house smells like garlic, tomatoes and basil. Spaghetti for dinner. The smell is distracting, so I get up and shut the sliding door. Mum pops her head in and tells us dinner will be soon. Dad says we'll pause it and watch the other half after dinner. We never had a TV at Sussex Street. Not actually connected. The no-TV decision was partly practical, as the aerial on the roof was broken. A compromise: dad said we would hire a TV and a VCR during the cold months, and just watch movies. Weird old movies. Dad, it turned out, was a cineaste.

Like most kids in the 1990s I was enthralled by action films and action film stars, especially the big five: Schwarzenegger, Bruce Willis, Stallone, Steven Seagal and Van Damme, followed closely by Dolph Lundgren, Chuck Norris and post-*Rumble in the Bronx* Jackie Chan. Movies like *Terminator 2* were passable as having artistic integrity, whereas anything starring Steven Seagal, Van Damme, Chuck Norris, or Lundgren had none. The basis for that discrimination come from on high and if I wanted to watch *Hard Target*, which I loved, I had to watch it at a friend's house. When the VCR came into the house it was for the contents of ACMI's lending library, which operated by post.

ACMI used to have a lending library that operated just like any other library but was done over the phone. Every week a thick cardboard box, taped shut with brown masking tape, was dispatched to the post office. Dad would pick up the ACMI parcel on the way home from his job at VicRoads call centre, headset on all day, then headset off and home. Depending on whether there was booze at home, he'd make a stop at the local bottle shop where he had credit. I like going into the bottle shop with him. There was a fish tank in the middle of the shop, hardboard polished beams overhead, and a cool slate floor.

The first Friday we did it I got to tear open the package and take the videos out. There's six in all. The first two are black and white. One is called *The General*, with a little guy being funny in front of a train on its cover. The little guy is Buster Keaton. The second one is a film that I'd learn was my dad's favourite. It's called *Rififi* and had some suave crook in a trenchcoat staring out from under his hat. Hands gloved but the right hand is un-gloved at the wrist, revealing a watch, and we know that time is important to this French thief. I pick it up and turn it over. Dad comes over to the dining table, taps the cover, and says what he'll say 100 times more in my life:

'It's got one of the best heist sequences in cinema.'

I look up at him, his thin face half shadowed by the kitchen light, and the dark outside. I had no idea what a heist sequence was. But I didn't want to ask. I wanted to find out for myself.

Friday nights were also fish and chips, and I always had a red lemonade with mine. Then, after our allocated weekly fast-food dinner, we would watch the film that had been chosen (most likely by me) for that evening. Sometimes my brother was there, but as he was two years older, and I was 11, he was often at his friend's house. Mum, Dad and I sat in our various spots: Mum in the big chair, left elbow bent on the wooden arm rest, the heel of her hand to her cheek, a pins and needles scenario; me sprawled on floor with my hands under my chin, pins and needles soon also, and away we'd go. Sometimes Dad would give us a packet of Maltesers, but Fantales with the hard caramel centre were my favourite.

I don't know where it came from, but we had a VHS that had two separate movies on the one cassette. At one end of the tape was *Rumble in the Bronx* then at the other end was a strange movie called *Four Rooms* where Tim Roth played a bellhop in a hotel, and every time he went into a different room, there was some crazy shit going on. That movie was cool, but we only watched that once cos it was rated MA15+ which meant I had to watch it with Mum and Dad. Mum loved a sequence of movies called *3 Colours Blue, 3 Colours Red* and *3 Colours White*. I tried to watch one of them but there was too much conversation I didn't understand. Dad let me watch *Apocalypse Now*, which I loved but it scared the shit out of me.

When we had the TV and VCR, I felt like we were a normal family, not different from what the other mums' and dads' houses were like at school. It was getting to the point where I didn't want to bring friends home and began timing bringing friends over during the TV-hiring months of winter. At the time we also drank purified water from a cask, and I didn't realise it was out of the ordinary. Then, I brought a friend over my house, taking the risk during a non-TV month; he didn't say anything about the no-TV, but when he saw the big cask of water he said:

'How come you're too poor to drink water, are you pilgrims?'

At the time it was a shock, calling my family poor (which we were) and even though I didn't know what a pilgrim was, it didn't sound good. My friend was Turkish and came from a religious background and I can only assume that he thought we were some kind of religious refugees, denouncing the modern world, forced to drink water out of box, with no TV.

At primary school, no one wanted to swap a packet of sultanas, which was our allocated sweet lunch box snack, for a packet of chips. We weren't allowed to get food from the canteen but saved up our allocated pocket money, $5 a week, and would splurge on dim sims and potato cakes. The best place to eat a potato cake was after a swim at Footscray Indoor Pool, which was like swimming in the heat of a greenhouse, without any plants. On numerous occasions I'd seen floating turds in the pool. But it had a waterslide, and we got around having to pay by climbing up into the mouth of the waterslide when the lifeguards weren't looking, getting as far up it as we could, before tumbling out.

Mum, a journalist and writer, who'd imposed the TV ban, must have even found the hiring TV months too much screen time, cos one day she came home with gifts for me and my brother: brand-new matching T-shirts that said KILL YOUR TV in big red and white letters inside a TV-sized square on the front. At the time everything we wore was from the op shop. The T-shirt had those tight sleeves and were short, 1970s style. Her timing was impeccable. After the pilgrim comment, and the T-shirt, and the fact that my older brother loved the T-shirt and wore it everywhere, I felt like an outsider in my family. I began to turn on my family. Up until that age, my brother and I had been close, but now, with his KILL YOUR TV T-shirt on, his skilful piano playing, his love of, and ability to comment on, my parents' musical tastes, while I sat there not knowing what they were talking about, made me feel like a stranger. At that age, apart from watching movies, I began to spend as little time at home as possible.

* * *

Dinner at Geoffrey and Lakshmi's place always started and ended the same way. We'd all be on the floor in their tiny St Kilda flat, eating rice and dahl with our hands, sitting on spread-out newspapers, Geoffrey, 50ish, with his big white feet with hair on his toes. Lakshmi, Geoffrey's second wife, small, golden brown, in a white and red chequered shawl around her face, gold bangles, gold nose ring, had been a servant for Geoffrey and Geoffrey's first wife back in Nepal, then had married Geoffrey after he brought her out to Australia with Lakshmi's daughter Mia, the only one of Lakshmi's three children to come to Australia.

After a few mouthfuls of rice and dahl, the bickering or aggressive mumbling and taunting would start. Lakshmi was twice illiterate, meaning she didn't read and write in her native language or in English, but would shake her head towards Geoffrey and in the most limited English would say:

'Geoffrey hitting, Geoffrey pushing.'

Geoffrey, with his deep voice, blue eyes, white dahl-flecked moustache, would tell Lakshmi to piss off. Mia in her early 20s, paler, round face, would hit Geoffrey on the head in a rough yet playful way. Dad and Mum thought all this was fine, but me and my brother, age six and eight, never got used to it. The whole scenario was so strange. I guess I probably thought it was funny. In the flat there were all sorts of stuff I'd never seen before. There was a trumpet that was made out of a human thigh bone; the knuckle of the bone was covered in woven leather and it made a sound like a cow mooing. There were bowls you dinged, and the noise stayed dinging for ages. After our weird dinners at Geoffrey's, we'd catch the light rail tram from St Kilda to Spencer Street, get the Werribee train home, and off at Yarraville. On the way home Mum and Dad didn't say anything about Geoffrey and Lakshmi except that they were always fighting.

Geoffrey's flat was in Grey Street. When we were going there it was the early-mid 90s. We were told not to stare, but there was so much to look at. There was always something happening. One time we met Geoffrey at an Italian restaurant near his flat, big garlic bread in baskets, photos of Calabria, red tablecloths, and we were sitting in the window when a scary-looking guy stopped in front of the window, stared right at us, pressed his face to the glass and banged on it. Geoffrey immediately stood up, went outside and I thought he was going to hit him, but he just had a stern word to him instead, like some kind of teacher. The wild guy just listened to him, as though he knew him.

Geoffrey was my mother's half-brother, child of their mother's first husband, twelve years older than her, ten older than dad, and he was a family legend, having returned to Australia after five years in London in the early1960s and then twenty years in Nepal. The story goes that Maria's second husband, and my mum's father, whose name was Geoff, set up young Geoffrey in a job and an apartment in London before they went home to Australia, maybe in advertising or something like that. Geoffrey hated it. So he left London and went to Nepal in the mid-60s, one of the first to take the hippie trail that went through Pakistan, Iran and India before eventually arriving in Kathmandu. He almost didn't make it to Kathmandu as he ran out of money in India and couldn't borrow money from family as they'd cut him off. In India, while flat broke, he ran into a friend from Australia who offered him an opportunity that was too good to pass up, importing and exporting goods and services all over the world. He made good money for a number of years, operating out of a shop in Kathmandu.

He was an intense man with a tobacco-stained white beard and clear blue eyes, which were amplified by the black turtlenecks he often wore, and he rode around St Kilda on an electric bike. Obsessed with sauna etiquette, Geoffrey enjoyed having arguments in the claustrophobic heat, and if they escalated into confrontations, well that was ok too. Dad began his own sauna career under Geoffrey's guidance. Given that he'd spent so long living in a high-altitude eastern environment, doing none of the tourist things, it felt like he'd earned the right to hold court on matters of etiquette and people listened. I can imagine that it must've been quite a shock for him coming home to the blandness of life in Melbourne after traversing potentially far more interesting territory for most of his life. Geoffrey's atmosphere was cool, and one where you paid attention, lest you miss a nugget of truth. In our family he was always spoken of with reverence. And of his three half-sisters, Mum was the closest to Geoffrey. He showed an interest. Which is how Dad and Geoffrey became good friends in the 1970s.

Apart from the few childhood memories, the only other encounter I had with Geoffrey was after I hadn't seen him for a decade or so. I was now 16 and I was invited over to join his inner sanctum, which basically consisted of smoking dope and talking. My brother, two years older, was already in. The first thing Geoffrey said when he saw me was how short I was, which I was already aware of. At the time, it put me on guard immediately. Why would someone of his age need to try and make a teenager feel even more awkward?

Once inside I think we smoked a joint and sat around. I got the feeling that the whole scenario was for Geoffrey's benefit; he was the wise old man, and everyone had to say the right thing. Punitive, but under the guise of relaxation, something like that. When he'd returned to Australia in the mid-1980s, he became a born-again Christian. He also subscribed to a magazine called *Nexus*, which pre-internet was the dominant platform on which all self-respecting conspiracy theorists communicated with each other.

I was overseas, checking emails at an internet café in Florence when I got word that Geoffrey had died. It was 2007. Geoffrey had lived with hepatitis since he was teenager; he'd contracted it from injecting amphetamines in the 1960s. He eventually got liver cancer and died of the complications of that, years later. As he was dying, there'd been a serious family get-together with his three half-sisters and my dad as Geoffrey didn't want to go into a hospice, he wanted family to take him in. But no one wanted the responsibility that came with caring for such an intense and difficult man at such a delicate time. So he went into a hospice that was part of St Vincent's Hospital and died there. Lakshmi and Mia had left Geoffrey years earlier and apart from my dad, he was alone.

It was strange that, for a man who I barely knew and had only met a handful of times, how upset I'd been at his death. At the time it felt as if my own yearlong overseas travel was the necessary apprenticeship that would grant me entry and acceptance from Geoffrey. Now that he was dead, I would never get that chance. I was crying openly, and heavily. As the tears slowed, I composed a eulogy. It was read out at his funeral on behalf of me and my cousins.

* * *

Ambrose Palmer Gym, located underneath the West Melbourne Stadium as it was known up until the 1980s, before being renamed Festival Hall, was a spiritual home for boxers in Melbourne. Up above, it was all glitzy grit as punters packed the stadium to watch boxers go to work for fifteen rounds under the bright lights, but the preparation for fifteen-round fights took place below the surface. And it was in the guts of the stadium where all the gruelling work was done, the relentless repetition, the pop, stick and move, the lick of the skipping rope on the hardwood floor, the slide and shuffle of boxers' feet on the canvas ring as they went to work under the watchful eye of Ambrose

Palmer. His boys were trained to use a specific style of fighting called The Method, a style that would eventually be known around the world in 1969 when one of his fighters, Johnny Famechon won a world title utilising The Method to perfection.

The Method was based on speed and more speed, hit and don't get hit, constant lateral movement, and always keeping the jab, pop pop, in the face of the opponent. If you were an orthodox fighter, the right hand, the power hand was used sparingly, as if the opponent is getting peppered with constant lefts, left jabs, left hooks, left rips to the body, then he won't be expecting the right hand, so when it does come, it's got the power, not just of the punch itself, but of by being hit by the punch that they didn't see coming, which, as they say, is the punch that does the damage. Until the opportune moment that right hand stayed glued to the chin. In sparring sessions, to keep the right hand in place, Ambrose would put a tie over Johnny Famechon's head, attached to the wrist like a sling, rendering that hand useless. It was a unique style created by the Palmers, who were a famous working-class family from Footscray.

But many years earlier, in the 1940s, long before Johnny Famechon put The Method on the map, a local welterweight training in the same gym was also being taught The Method in its more rudimentary form. His boxing name was Jackie Daniels, his real name was Percival Hubert Freeman, and he was married to my Yvonne, my great-aunt. There was real pride in my dad's family, and this was displayed literally, by the prominence on the mantlepiece of a black and white photo of Jackie Daniels, taken in the classic boxing pose. As a kid I would ask my dad who he was and he'd say the Victorian Welterweight Champion in 1943, Rose's sister's husband. I never met him, and he died before I was born.

The prestige of winning a Victorian title might not seem that great these days, but back then, when there were upwards of 150 or so boxers in a similar weight division in the same area, you had your work cut out for you. And according to the *Argus* newspaper, with my own little add-ons, his win went something like this.

It's 1943 and the West Melbourne Stadium is packed with characters of all sorts. Men in their knit shirts, vests, pullovers, sport coat ensembles, sweaters, high pants. The women in hats, slim-waisted in skirts below the knee, gloves, dainty bags, overcoats. Tonight a new Victorian welterweight champion would be crowned, and Melbourne boxing fans are out in force to see the local boys in action.

Terry Reilly, real name William Terrence Gunn, is the older of the two fighters. By 1943 he'd fought his way through two weight divisions, having won a state championship at super lightweight, a state welterweight championship, and also an Australian welterweight championship in 1941. Reilly is no slouch. He's also a heavy hitter and it's a sure bet he'll swing away down the stretch. But what Reilly doesn't anticipate is how easily a little-known local fighter, Jackie Daniels, could move in behind an open right glove, blocking Reilly's effective punches, the straight 1–2. But, by the middle of the seventh round, Jackie is smothering his own work to protect himself after getting clipped with a left hook, and by the end of the eighth, both men are unwilling to open up, and the crowd is restless. Jackie's never been in a fifteen-round fight, and by the middle of the ninth his eye is badly cut, and he's gone into his shell. The trend continues in the ninth. They clinch again and both boxers rummage for coins in each other's pockets. But who's gonna make the KO call from within the phone-booth where they're fighting? Reilly's against the ropes and Jackie has an opening. He takes it, not with both hands, but with one, a perfectly timed right hook to the body. Reilly doubles over, rolls onto his back, staggers up, just beating the count. By now, the phone is ringing off the hook. So when Reilly continues, Jackie answers, speaks loud and clear, then slams it down with another right hook in the same spot. When he lands it, Reilly doesn't make the count. The crown is passed. The phone rings for only one man, Jackie Daniels.

He went on to have eighty-two fights, winning thirty (only six by KO), losing forty-seven; five were a draw. He retired from boxing in 1951. He worked as a bouncer in various pubs and clubs. He also had a stint as a tent boxer in Jimmy Sharman's Boxing Troupe when they came to the Royal Melbourne Show. Jimmy Sharman or Jimmy Jnr on the megaphone, drawing in the punters.

'Who'll take a glove? A pound or two for a round or two.'

Along the way he made enough money from boxing to buy a house that he turned into a milk bar. Business in front and live out the back. It was in Tottenham, next to the freight yard.

* * *

Yarraville West Primary School is a long, two-storey brick block at 30 Powell Street Yarraville. Traditionally, the school was divided into two sides: girls on one side, boys on the other. And when the 1950s post-war boom brought European migrants to Yarraville, a heavily industrial area at the time, the families sent their kids to either Yarraville Primary, a school that closed in 1994, Wembley Primary on the border of Yarraville and Kingsville, or to Yarraville West Primary School. The school was about 60 per cent white Anglo; the other 40 per cent was ethnically mixed, with Vietnamese, Chinese, Turkish, Macedonian, Greek, Croatian, Tongan, Fijian, and Indigenous Australian kids.

By the time I started there in 1993 the school was still divided, but into small school and big school, with prep to Grade 3 on one side, and Grades 4–6 on the other. The kids on the little school side had a small area to play in. There was a sandpit with tarps over it, a tanbark-chip playground, and large, low-hanging trees with sticky leaves that were covered in tiny peppercorns.

The school's emblem was two lines down and two lines across, essentially a four-squared game of noughts and crosses in a closed circle. It was above the entry to the school in electric blue. Once inside the school the emblem changed colour and size, becoming a giant white hollow metal sculpture, and acted as the backdrop in the faded brick amphitheatre, in front of which Sharon, the principal, with her short grey hair, blue jeans and brown RM Williams would, hand on heart, sing the national anthem at assembly every morning at 8.55.

I arrived at Yarraville West in Grade 2 and was only on the little side for two years till I crossed over to the big school, via the long concrete walkway that went up and over the assembly area, down past the old blue doors, past the multi-purpose hall, the big kids' toilets, inside of which the ceilings were covered with so many chunky toilet paper spit balls that it looked like a science experiment, and onwards, out past the big kids' canteen, and into the forecourt and beyond that was a big playground, basketball court and handball court. And right down the end of the school grounds was a wide-open grassy area split in two by a line of trees running up the middle where we played British Bulldogs.

Anyone who wanted to could play British Bulldogs. It was a very simple game. The bulldog or bulldogs (depending on the size of the playing field, in this case a large grassy area) start off in the middle, yell out 'British Bulldogs', which is the cue for the rest of the players, who are on the starting line, to run from one side to the other without getting grabbed (it was a physical game, aggressive, as players were tackled to the ground) by the bulldogs in the middle. Every time a player is taken down, they're added to number of bulldogs in the middle, till eventually there's only player left, and that last player is the winner. We played British Bulldog with upwards of twenty kids sometimes, and the slow kids got tackled into the trees and slammed on the ground. I was small and evasive, often the last to run the gauntlet through the line of kids standing at various spots. A few years later schools banned British Bulldogs cos some kid got brain damage when he got slammed to the deck.

If we weren't playing British Bulldogs, we played a game, that, in retrospect, I have no idea how we came across it. We called it the Fainting Game and it went like this. One kid stood facing a wooden fence down at the grassy area. He exhaled all the oxygen from his lungs. Then once it was gone, whoever was behind him pushed him up against the fence, forcing every last drop of air out of his body, causing him to faint. The other two kids acted as catches. And when the kid fainted, he was caught under the arms. It was pretty exhilarating. I played the Fainting Game with Ivan, Steve, Emir and Duck.

He was a cool kid. He was one of my best friends at Yarraville West Primary. His family owned a milk bar in Footscray. I never saw his mum without a ciggy, specifically a Peter Jackson super mild. The packet was the colour of a blue summer sky. His mum and dad were separated, but his dad was always around. Baba this, baba that; he wore lots of gold, and white linen shirts, open at the neck, had a husky voice. Emir had a little brother and a baby sister.

It's the weekend and I'm on the roof of the Footscray Primary School, near Emir's house, with Des, Emir's friend, and we're smashing up the tiles. It's a small bluestone school with high pointed spires and a large, sloped, ceramic-tiled roof, and we've climbed up and we're in the dip, where you can walk one foot in front of the other. The tiles are big and heavy; I can only hold one of them at a time, but I use all the force my little body can muster and bring it down hard, smashing a big hole in the roof. When I step back, I see that there's now a larger hole, and inside it's some kind of roof cavity. I stick my head in. It's a small attic, and for some reason, is full of heaps of Apple computers, the off-green-coloured ones the size of a small birdcage with the floppy disk drive in front. They were in every school classroom in the mid-90s.

When Emir and I became close friends, Mum suggested I ride my bike to his house from Yarraville to West Footscray. But I hated my bike. It had a weird frame (potentially girlish) and looping metal handlebars like giant insect antennae, with no grip. I refused to ride it and started going there on public transport, two train stations from Yarraville to Footscray, then I'd either get the 82 tram half a dozen stops, or if there was no tram I'd walk. I was getting further and further away from my family. I just wanted to keep on going. By age 11 I'd saved up months of pocket money and could finally buy the outfit I'd wanted for so long. A yellow and blue Nike tracksuit. And when I had it, I never took it off. I needed shoes to go with it, and for Christmas that year I got a pair of Nike Air Max Triax. I wore this outfit everywhere. To school, and defiantly to family events, whenever I left the house. Just me and my banana tracksuit.

I took my tracksuited self to Highpoint and spent most of my time playing Time Crisis, a first-person shooter game I loved. The game's gimmick was a foot pedal you utilised to hide and reload, which was different from the other shooting games like Virtual Cop and House of the Dead, where you had to shoot offscreen to reload. Time Crisis was a tactile experience. The quicker you were to shoot accurately, hide and reload, the quicker you clocked the level. One minute to blast your way through campy villains in trucker caps and moustaches, with extra seconds added to your clock the more risks you took, avoiding the crisis of time.

In 1997 Crown Casino was the new kid on the block, and Emir and Des and I wanted to get acquainted with it. We came up with the most basic of plans: get the last train to the city with money in our pockets and take it from there. Not long after coming up with this master plan, we're waiting at Footscray Station for the last train, acting like it was the most important thing in the world. To enhance the importance, before we got on the train, we smoked a ciggy each while classical music flowed out of the train station speakers. A bizarre attempt to reduce crime on public transport that seemed to last only a few years. I wonder how many budding teenage criminals pissing in train carriages and smashing windows were inspired to put down a rock and pick up a cello? When the train came, we sat down the end of the carriage, conspiratorial, avoiding the loud men and women at the other end.

We got off the train at Spencer Street and Des, a massive 12-year-old Tongan, took the lead. Emir and I either side. V formation. We walked down the hill towards the river, went underneath the train bridge, and continued straight, across the river. About halfway over the bridge, we saw the simulated fireballs that would burst out of these big black concrete slabs on the waterfront like a sideshow gimmick on the promenade, and as though trapped in the flash of a primal photograph, we stood still, watching as they scorched the night, sizzling our cocoons with enough razzle dazzle that we basically flew the rest of the way to Crown.

When we got inside, we felt special walking across the red carpeted glass tunnels with the drunk girls in short skirts, thick men in cheap suits. On the way to the 24-hour arcade called Galactic Circus located at the back of Crown, with three levels of wall-to-wall games. Cashiers wearing little vests, enough fluorescents to make Chinatown jealous. Emir and Des went one way, I went another, and out of habit, went straight for Time Crisis 2. They always played that basketball game, which I thought was lame. You could just play basketball any time, so why play it here? We thought we'd brought lots of money, but it was probably like $20 each. Emir had more, maybe $50, cos he stole money from his milk bar till. Either way, it ran out quick. After that, we didn't know what to do; no other plan. Des, our leader, had strict religious parents and was terrified of them, and he said we should go home. Me and Emir didn't want to go home. Des kicked up a fuss and stormed off, but without any more money, we caught him up, and began walking in the general direction of home.

By the 1990s the Docklands area had become a massive derelict sprawl of empty warehouses, obsolete infrastructure, an abandoned waterfront. The main cause of the area's 'decline' was the mechanisation of industry; specifically containerisation, when the metal boxes jampacked with goods and stacked on ships were delivered more efficiently with minimal human involvement. Prior to the change, it was longshoremen who did most of the work. Crews of men did the unloading and loading, labour that was an integral part of the Port of Melbourne's extensive network of wharfs, heavy rail and industry had been replaced and, in the process, emptied out the people, changed the character of port cities not just in Melbourne, but all over the world. By the late 1990s the Victorian Government had begun reinvesting in the area and began building the sports stadium. And to get to Footscray Road to begin our long walk home from the city, we had to walk right past the gigantic concrete beginnings of Docklands Stadium. It was far too irresistible to not get in and see what all the fuss was about.

Cos I was the smallest I wedged myself between the chain link fence and pushed a section of the fence apart so that Des and Emir could get in. From the fence we walked straight in. I remember walking around in a semi-circle, as only one side had been built. Running, jumping, drifting through the cavernous place. Emir ran along with me, Des sort of jogged; he wanted to get out as soon as we got in, thinking of the belting he'd get if his folks knew he'd snuck out. Sprinting then slowing down. Feeling the massiveness of it. The cool quiet from an echo stretched around the corners, bounced around for a bit before coming back. We went to look at where the turf would be laid. An alien place waiting to be inhabited. A place that in the coming years would be alive with boisterous activity, but back then was as silent as a graveyard. We got lost, and after a while, found our way out and began the long walk home.

All the way home, along the long stretch of Footscray Road, the only people we saw zoomed past high up behind big truck windshields. A worker in the service station we walked past when we were halfway home, a miniature behind glass underneath a tent of blinding light. We kept moving, smoked, walked, talked. Over the other side of the road a sudden buzz of activity. Forklifts pinging around, the Melbourne Wholesale Fruit and Veg Market warming up. Even though the sun was still a few hours away, it was spring and we were also warming up. An hour so later we crossed the bridge over the Maribyrnong River, walked through the shuttered and empty Footscray streets to West Footscray, where Emir and Des lived. Our first stop was Des's house, and we should've been quieter. As he was climbing in his window, a light went on, his dad's voice boomed, and we ran, leaving Des to get the belting of his life. Emir's mum had no idea that we were even there in the first place, and didn't notice us coming back in.

* * *

Steve was a good Greek boy from a good Greek house. His mum was a teacher and his old man worked for the union. He was a brown-eyed, rosy-cheeked kid who looked after his grandma and did his chores dutifully. A teenybopper like me. Steve's family lived in a large weatherboard house in Seddon.

Ivan was Croatian and had a big blond head with blue eyes, was a bit dopey, and liked wearing knee-length shorts with white socks and skate shoes, listened to *Frenzal Rhomb* and *Millencolin*. A good footballer. Was game for whatever. He lived with his mum, older sister, and a stepdad he didn't get along with, in Yarraville. His Dad lived in Deer Park.

When I moved away from Yarraville, I lost touch with Duck and didn't see him again, not like Ivan and Steve, who I saw every now and then. To me, he was still the kid with the cowlick who bum sucked his ciggies, and the kid who one day brought a box of Granny Smiths dipped in glorious red toffee, toffee apples, to school for a fete or something, and we ate most of them.

Steve went to Williamstown High then got a degree in advertising. For a time he worked in one of those bright and airy office spaces where they play ping-pong and troubleshoot ideas, but he was quietly developing an ice habit, and when his dad died, he went in hard; his use spiralled into dealing, then trafficking. He's currently serving three years for a botched home invasion.

Ivan's descent into drugs and crime was foreseeable, given that his old man would let him smoke ice at the kitchen table when he was still in high school. He also made the national news in 2014 when cops raided his house and found a huge stockpile of stolen copper. Along the way he'd gotten so good at Graff that he's now a living Melbourne legend in the scene.

I didn't see Emir for a number of years, then I heard he'd teamed up with Anthony, another childhood friend and early Graff companion. Both boys were under the tutelage of a Serbian heroin dealer who operated out of the Palms Motel in Footscray. Both boys became junkies and are in and out of jail.

Duck went to Footscray City College and got really into steroids. Then in 2011 he popped up on the news after being charged as an accessory to the bashing murder of a backpacker at pub in Yarraville. He disappeared after turning Crown witness at the trial.

I'm not really sure why so many of my childhood friends from the western suburbs went on to have such troubled lives. But it makes sense if you combine a lack of opportunity for employment after the decimation and collapse of the working classes with shit fathers and mothers with no time outside of work, throw drugs and crime in, and finally, gentrification, as the last nail in the coffin, killing any spirit that was left of the old inner west.

8
Fights
Undercard. Main Event. KO.

UNDERCARD

One of the first punches I ever threw was a real coward's punch and I broke a knuckle on my right hand in the process. I was with Lil Chris. We were at a party in Moonee Ponds. It was 2002. I was 16 and also tiny for my age, hadn't had my teenage growth spurt, basically looked 13. Lil Chris wasn't little any more. He'd gone from Lil C to Big C overnight, no longer liked being called Lil Chris. No-one called him that any more, lest they got punched in the face.

I don't know how we ended up at this particular party cos I think the only person I knew there was an acquaintance of an acquaintance, something like that, definitely not a crowd I knew. The house seemed to be full of sporty geeks wearing fedora hats, racing bikes on hooks in the hallway, Tibetan prayer flags hung over the porch. We got sideways looks as soon as we entered. At the time, I went to parties to steal. And that's what I did, grabbed a wallet on a bookshelf, dacked it and walked out, but was spotted, and as we walked out through the front gate, two sporty geeks bailed us up. The leader wore a *Matrix* coat and a red fedora; his mate wore some weird denim ensemble.

Prior to that night I'd had a few schoolyard scuffles, headlocks, footy shoving, etc, never thrown a legit punch, but as I stood there on the footpath, anticipatory, I thought, how hard could it be? I denied everything, turning out both hands and my pockets, like what? His mate in the denim ensemble said it was down my pants. Lil Chris laughed and called him a fag. Meanwhile, other sporty geeks piled out on to the porch and were yelling now. A blonde girl wearing a dress over jeans, a furry jacket and some kind of scarf, screamed at us from the porch, her gravelly rich-girl voice jolting the air, jolting all of us, and, like some kind of call to action, I flexed my right hand at the sound, lunged two steps under the cover of the jolt, past Lil Chris, and punched the fedora guy on the left side of his face, up near the cheek, I think. He stumbled back, while at the same time, as though the whole scene was one continuous slow-motion sequence, I saw stars as his denim ensemble friend, who I'd deemed a useless goose, had punched me in the side of the head. I went sideways, there were noises from everywhere, then over the rustle and yelling came a loud crack, followed by a man squealing, and I saw Lil Chris laying into the friend. The fedora was on the grass; the porch geeks were coming at us. I gathered myself, grabbed Lil Chris and we ran, and kept running out of the street, on to the road, then we slowed. I had a lump on my left cheek but nothing major, Lil Chris was all pumped up, had blood on his white T-shirt, wasn't his. I'd forgotten about the wallet, our prize, but when I checked and there was only $30, I didn't really give a shit. I took the cash and threw the rest away.

I'd never considered myself someone who 'punched on', I was just Dom the sneak thief or the guy who stole stuff from parties, but after that night, in my head, the image of a fighter, or someone who would fight, became part of who I thought I was. I think I told the story of that night a hundred times, relishing the thrill, reliving the event, how it sounded, how it made me feel.

MAIN EVENT

I'm 26, flying on coke on King Street in the early hours of the morning, walking alongside Tom, my drug-addled companion, and I'm slightly disoriented, not from the drugs, but cos so much of the street I remembered wasn't the same. Yet even in its tamer, lamer, shadow-of-former-self-state, King Street still retained the sleazy, potential-for-violence atmosphere. I still got high, tried to pick up girls, and punched on every now and then. I enjoyed dancing to cheesy hip hop and RnB, Rihanna, Beyonce.

The street is hot and heavy, it's February. We weave among girls wearing short leather skirts, animal-print leggings, trainers. I'm confused cos the guys look kinda like the girls, who wear bucket hats, ironic T-shirts, and lots of gold. We pass a backpacker hostel near the corner of Bourke Street and King, and out the front is a bunch of guys wearing matching Hawaiian shirts, all pumped up, holding warm-looking Bacardi Breezers, a delegation of boofheads; half of them have white iPod earphones, so bright they seem to glow in the dark. There's no actual breeze, no wind. Sticky, stagnant city. The mix of cocaine, booze and the street has gone to my head. We cross over Bourke and head down the hill, following the ancient flow of shit. Over Collins Street and into the flesh market section, Spearmint Rhino, Showgirls Bar 20, but we're on the opposite side of the street. Better view from here.

Movement catches my eye from the other direction. I see him, walking up the hill, 50 or so metres away. He's in his forties, bald and shirtless, wearing trainers, shorts. As he gets closer, I swear I can see the neon reflections off his slick bald dome. He's about 20 metres away, yelling abuse at everyone, having a great time.

First sequence: Shirtless neon thug in his forties wearing trainers and shorts, walking in our direction.

Second sequence: Missing. A blank gap.

Third sequence: I'm half in the gutter and half on the footpath and it would seem, given where my body is, that I've been speartackled to the ground and baldie has my arms pinned. Neon baldie is strong, but also one-dimensional, hell bent on his wrestling/burrowing technique, but if he keeps burrowing and digging, he's gonna rebirth himself right through me. Street orchestra in full swing, yelling, bunches of legs shuffling at eye level, car horns blare and clang, symbols crash together, and it's like a cooked conductor has gone berserk with their musical baton. Tom was half in the gutter too and had gotten his leg wedged under him, stuck. I'm battling to keep the back of my head from smashing on the concrete. I flex as much as I can, giving me just enough space to weasel my arms out, and when I get my full wingspan back, I unleash haymakers left and right, cracking hooks till his body goes limp.

Fourth sequence: I'm out of the gutter, in a doorway, shirtless. I could've sworn I was wearing at least two layers of clothes. How did I get to the doorway? I see him, wearing shorts and trainers, crouched in a shop doorway nearby. Blood dripping down his face, his upper body being attended to by paramedics. When did they arrive? There's people everywhere. I move towards him trying get a better look. Confusion intensifying when I see the guy who only a moment ago was trying to enter my abdomen using the most aggressive hug I've ever had. I start yelling at him, half abuse, half questions. Who are you, what the fuck did I do to you? I don't get any closer to him cos the background crackles into the foreground and two beefy cops corral me, push me back to the doorway.

Fifth sequence: The cops are telling me to shut the fuck up, to stop yelling on the street dickhead, cos look, we're gonna let you go with a fine. And even though I was the other half of the offence, they're saying he had a knife and had been involved in other incidents leading up to this. I didn't see the knife, but they reckon it spilled out in the fight. Tom had disappeared, but came away with a broken ankle, ended up spending the next few months walking around in a moonboot. I broke my right thumb on the psycho's head, and sent him off in an ambulance, and the cops were celebrating my achievements, yeah look at his face, you smashed him, etc. I saw him on a stretcher, lights flashing, nothing to see here, a fight on King Street about as regular as a bowel movement. The coke had worn off. I didn't have any more, so I hailed a cab home.

KO

I stopped going to gigs in my early twenties for a variety of reasons, but mainly cos they were boring, so it was a bit of an anomaly that I ended up at Festival Hall to see Lauryn Hill, with Nas as special guest, in 2019 at age 33. To be fair, my cousin had a free ticket otherwise I wouldn't've gone. I'd never been to Festival Hall, just passed it on the train, in and out of the western suburbs since I was a kid.

As soon as we step inside, I immediately regret being there and have to remind myself that I'm not 18 years old. Looking around, we've truly stepped into a time tunnel. And the heads who've never left the tunnel are now kings, gold-toothed, gold-chained, gold standard. The women have aged better. Late 30s early 40s, who've been in the scene since the jump but have branched out, lived lives beyond drugs and local rivalries, sexy outfits, short skirts, big gold hoop earrings. Me and my cousin get drinks, find a spot, dance a bit, drink some more. After a little while I have to take a break from it. I go outside for a cigarette.

There aren't that many people outside. I walk over to the fence, roll and light a ciggy. I watch the traffic coming into North Melbourne via Docklands from the left, and from Footscray Road to the right, passing below. Trains clunk by on the bridge above, and the freight and V-line train yard spreads its tracks out in a row. Directly over the whoosh of traffic is an army-green-coloured building with dirty old windows. Grime-gunked portholes into an ancient locker room. I see an old green locker has been left open, a yellowy glow surrounded by darkness. Looking into the grimy room, I imagine a wandering trainyard spirit waiting for the locker to be closed so it can finally go home. I hear a noise behind me, and a guy suddenly right next to me like the ghost from across the way.

'Got a ciggy bud?'

He's got a face like one of my great-uncles in a photo from a backyard piss-up in the 1960s, bright eyes, collapsed cheeks, hair slicked and flicked to the side, but the modern tracksuit version. I tell him:

'Yeah, rollies but?'

He's just asked for a ciggy. His simple question creates an immediate ripple effect through my body. After he's rolled the ciggy, there's no more talk. He just stands there. I have nothing to say. The internal tension could be cos I can't pretend to respect men in the same way I used to.

'I'm heading in. Have a good night aye.'

Locker room ghost replies, 'You too lad.'

Done. Inside to find my cousin.

Nas comes on and does 'Got Yourself a Gun'. If I wasn't drunk, it'd be a lot harder to pretend I'm interested. Propelled by a hard-to-place anxiety, we push closer to the stage. Rolling with the crowd. Then I get whiplash from a hard shove in the back. I sprawl awkwardly. It's not an accident. I gather myself, turn around to see who did it. A lanky fuck with a neck tattoo is smiling at me. Immediately I push him back, then my cousin steps between us. We scuffle. Security comes over, breaks it up. The fuckhead and his fuckhead mate disperse, as do me and my cousin. We go outside and go for a walk.

I hadn't been in a fight, or anything resembling a fight, for years, and now I was back in the game like I'd never left. Overwhelmed, now all I wanted was revenge. Electric brain buttons fizzed to life. Atavistic wiring lighting up a dark runway in my mind. I try to cool my head, but I can't. My cousin and I circle back round to the exit of Festival Hall. I try to distract myself, but the plane has landed. I squint over at the exit. I see him come out. On reflex, as though nothing has changed in two decades, I move towards him from across the wide road. Each stride, each beat, brings me closer to the past. Gaining momentum. I'm within a half dozen strides of my slow-motion attack when I realise that he's well over 6ft. I didn't notice earlier. I keep going. The road dips into a concave. My last image is running towards him, full sprint, bright lights reflecting off the exterior of Festival Hall, 10 metres and brighter, 5 metres and brightest, lunging upwards out of the concave, last image. Snap.

* * *

The Alfred Hospital. Two cops asking me questions. I'm being aggressive. I try to voice my aggression, but it comes out like a dribble, not physical dribble, but there's an obvious disconnect between what I think I'm doing and what I'm actually doing. Not coherent. The cops make me aware of this. They tell me to relax and that I've been the victim of a serious assault. And I've been unconscious for an hour or so. They tell me I was kicked unconscious, kicked in the head. My face is badly grazed, my nose, my chin, I'm all bandaged up. I tell everyone passing me in the hospital, whether it's a nurse, a doctor, a civilian, that I wish to go home now, look I'm fine. I talk in long-winded nonsense, until I'm told to please be quiet. I apologise. The cops can't get anything useful out of me. Where's my cousin? I check my phone. It's packed with missed calls and texts from him.

Neck Tatt was arrested and charged with assault and grievous bodily harm. My cousin gave a statement, but Neck Tatt's friend also gave a statement, and it became his word against my cousin's. For whatever reason, I refused to make a statement, and the cops couldn't do anything about it. I'm given more painkillers and drop off to sleep. I wake. A doc is assessing me. She's saying my eyes are clear, and the scan they did upon arrival showed no worrying signs. I'm ok to leave.

I walk out of the hospital of my own volition into the quiet morning and the air is so still it's like the park across the road is all glass. A fox enters the frame, shattering the moment. Runs off into the park. I shudder. I walk towards the servo up at the intersection. I hail a passing cab, but he pulls away when he sees my bandaged-up head. The next one accepts me. I'm very, very thankful. In the back seat of the cab, I look out the window and all I can hear is the sound of the car and the throb in my head. The landscape emptied out. Empty petrol stations. Empty train stations. Empty streets. Empty everything.

9
Spiralling in Stream C
Slow Days in the Newstart Alcove

I'm late for my appointment at Max Employment and the puffy-eyed receptionist clicks her tongue at my tardiness then gestures with a fake-tanned hand to a section of the office where I see a semi-circle of fellow long-term chronically unemployed individuals, grouped together. Rodney will be running today's session. I've met him a few times. He's one of those guys who wears jeans and hiking shoes and is constantly invigorated by life and enjoys keeping people on edge with the thought that he could potentially go off-road at any moment.

His story, I heard last session, is that he arrived in St Kilda in 1994 with nothing but his bass guitar and his dreams, but he had to sell his guitar and his dreams to Cash Converters and give up a future as a musician, cos the cover band he played bass with wasn't working out. So, he made the wise and realistic decision to get a job and be happy. He's draining and overly self-conscious but compared to Pamela – the platinum-blonde conservative motivational speaker who gave us a pep talk a few months ago, after which I felt like my face muscles had been blown back as if I'd been facing an airplane engine – Rodney is manageable. The Progress Alcove, a.k.a. Rodney's Palace, is like being trapped on a square of old carpet in an Officeworks basement.

To my left in the semi-circle is Gary, a morbidly obese teenager who must be only just out of school. His speech is slow, as if he has an acquired brain injury. His long black hair obscures most of his face. His feet are in sandals, which are the same colour as his black trackies.

When we introduce ourselves, Gary tells us that he just wants to build computers at home cos that keeps him calm. Next to Gary is Melanie, mid-twenties, dyed blonde hair, very thin. She mostly stares at her phone. A tattoo that says Respect, in cursive font, is visible on the inside of her wrist. To my right is John. He must be at least sixty. He's dressed well, as though this session is a job interview. His greying hair is parted and flat to his head. He's wearing a crisp blue shirt, black pants and black shoes. He looks like he's already gotten the job, whatever that job may be. He's sipping instant coffee from a styrofoam cup.

Rodney produces a little blue bouncy ball from his pocket. He proceeds to bounce it up and down on the carpet. I'm sitting the closest to him. I think about grabbing it, turning the tables and putting him in the chair while I bounce the ball off his head. Instead, we hypnotically follow its bounce. I imagine a 'very significant' memo in circulation among the managers of the Job Service Providers with the title 'Ball Games and Barriers':

To address the specific needs of Job Seekers, I hereby declare all ball games, with all variations of balls (volley, tennis, football, soccer, basketballs, etc.) to be implemented into the dynamic structures of Job Service Providers Procedure.

Sincerely,
Matt

The ball hits the inside of Rodney's palm with a little slap and this sound causes Melanie to look up at Rodney. 'Oi, what day is it?'

Rodney pretends not to hear Melanie, but half the office can hear Melanie. Gary looks worried, staring down at his feet. John hasn't flinched. Melanie jerkily stands up. 'I only got outta hospital yesterday!

Rodney closes his eyes. 'Look Melanie, we all have to be here. We can't have it all.'

'Yeah, but I've got another appointment. I've gotta see my doctor.'

'What time?

'Now.'

Rodney squeezes the ball. 'You won't get paid if you leave.'

Melanie steps it up. 'Fuck this!

Gary and John remain silent. Rodney is squeezing the ball so tight that his hand is going white.

'Fukin laterz.'

Melanie storms out. The speed at which she moves through the stagnant office creates a rush of wind in her wake that sends a pile of papers crashing to the floor. Rodney is momentarily flustered. He smooths out his shirt, smiles awkwardly.

'Are we all ok?'

Nobody says anything. I look at the clock. We've only been here for ten minutes.

'Dominic, are we ok?'

He says 'we' in that passive-aggressive way to try and make me think we are all in this together. A team. Gary is still looking down. John is a blank. I answer in well-practised monotone, 'Yes, we are all ok.'

Everyone involved with a Job Service Provider has a classification from A–D. I'm classified as a Stream C, which in Centrelink's language officially translates to 'a person who has a combination of vocational and non-vocational issues that need to be addressed before they can take up and retain a job', or unofficially, to *'this person is a burden to us all, and all we can do is hopefully add weight to their unfortunate situation, crush them even more, so that hopefully they'll be too depressed to attend appointments therefore we can lawfully suspend their payments indefinitely'*. To be put on Stream C, I was thoroughly assessed by a Centrelink worker like a suspect under questioning. I was deemed to be a legitimately malfunctioning unit.

***

Back when I'd only been unemployed for a year or so (pre-long term) I was dedicated to doing what I had to do to live off their extremely punitive payment. To beat them at their own game. I lived in a tiny room in a seven-person share house owned by the Portuguese Catholic Church next door. The rent was cheap. My room was 3x3 metres. And my bed was where a bath used to be. The Newstart payment then (up until May 2020) was $250 a week. So, after rent, which was $120, I had $130 for bills, food and transport for the week. That's $18 a day. Try giving that a crack. Once a week for the past three years I'd steal all my groceries from the supermarket. And not that crusty dumpster diving shit. I didn't scavenge around in the dark in the hope of finding something substantial before ending up with a carton of baby food that would be shared by some bourgeois anarchists in Coburg. I went in during the day and took what I wanted. I stole so I could be as independent as possible. I'd fill up two green bags' worth of necessities. Meat, vegetables, fruit, bread, milk, butter, spaghetti, coffee, etc. I had a shopping list, which was essential, but also made me look more legit. I did everything calmly and openly. I liked to maintain a low heart rate. I waited till the timing was right. When someone walked in the doors that swung open, I'd walk right past them. I'd look straight ahead. I'd be gone. This saved me around $80–$100 a week. If I hadn't stolen $100 worth of groceries every week and cooked big bolognaise, big soups, big everything with my stolen food, then I wouldn't have been able to live on the money at all.

Back in the Progress Alcove Rodney has written something on the whiteboard. It says, Early Job Seekers Catch the Employment Worm. He taps it with a blue whiteboard marker,

'What time do we think is a good time to get up in the morning?'

No one says anything. Tap, tap. He scans the group and his eyes linger on John, the only hope. After an agonising amount of time, he speaks.

'I'd say that 7 am is a good time to rise.'

Rodney crouches down and gives John a high five, which John reciprocates. Gary interjects.

'An employment worm sounds like a disease?'

Rodney doesn't think it's funny.

'And Gary, what time do you get up?'

Gary looks at all of us, hoping for a friendly face. I give him one.

'Whenever I wake up.'

'But that's not going help you get a job, is it?'

A pause. Gary is thinking seriously about something, before looking directly at Rodney.

'But I don't think I can get a job.'

The progress alcove constricts. Oxygen becomes scarce. John sips audibly. Gary is taking the initiative, addressing the elephant in the room, and Rodney is taken off guard. Gary continues, 'Have you got any jobs where I can build computers?'

'I'm not sure if there's a job where you can do that, Gary. But how about a job working on a computer at a call centre or something?'

Gary shakes his head. I look down, hoping to be passed over, but I don't get away that easily.

'Dominic, you've been quiet. What kind of employment do you have in mind?'

The trick is, say you want a job that is basically unattainable, like being a pilot. But sometimes I accidentally tell the truth.

'I've been trying to write some things down that I might turn into a story.'

I'm trying to piece together the events that have led me to be here in this room with an old man trapped in 1989, a kid with an acquired brain injury, and a girl struggling to survive. I've been drifting for years but I don't want to drift any more.

I need to get out of the tiny room. I'm thirsty. I need a drink of water. I better move fast before John drinks the whole cooler dry. Outside the room I see the flattening compression of space, ideal for supreme surveillance. The Job Service Providers Officers Playground is a hotbed of CCTV-inspired paranoiacs. They watch each other. Zooming in. Zooming out. Voyeuristically sussing out co-workers' performance levels. Office secrets divulged to privileged parties in encrypted messaging sessions. Flattening of space. Flattening of heads. I look at John and think that maybe he is right after all. The water is poisoned. Rodney has taken a call in the Bluetooth in his ear. He presses the earpiece like a secret agent and starts talking. He nods to me as I make a drinking gesture and point to the cooler. On my way I ask John, 'How's the water in this place?'

He looks at me as though I'm somewhere far off in the distance. His eyes flicker.

'I reckon they poison it.'

The government has allocated $7.5 billion for employment over the past five years and I bet not a single cent of that money will be going towards keeping people in long-term suitable employment. Max Employment is owned by Maximus, an American multinational corporation that posted $1.7 billion in profit in 2014. Where does all the money go? Most of it goes to meddling middle managers whose job it is to manage the non-middle managers to make sure those up-and-coming managerial positions are being properly managed. Who else is gonna manage the situation?

'Alrighty, time's almost up.'

Rodney claps and we all look around as though emerging from a cave. Gary was sleeping with his head on his chest, but at the clap, his head snaps up. He rubs his eyes. Rodney, another successful session ticked off, hands out a form with questions on it. There are stick figures performing various emotions on the form, so if your literacy levels aren't crash hot, you know what to say. Question: how often do you feel hopeless? Is it, 1 – never, 2 – occasionally, 3 – sometimes, 4 – often or 5 – all the time? At the end of the question, a stick figure sits with its head in its hands. Its little stick figure tears drop to the floor.

John loves the water in this place, so I let him go first at the cooler. He refills, then I do and Gary does too. We all stand there in a semi-circle, drinking. A door whooshes open and Melanie storms back in. She yells at the receptionist, 'I need to be marked off.'

Eyes look up over computers, noses twitch, office rabbits assess threat level then back in the hole.

Rodney appears to calm the storm and Melanie turns on him, but he is used to this. He's got the bouncy ball in his hand again. He bounces it next to his ready-for-action hiking shoes on the grey carpet in front of Melanie. On the third bounce he closes his hand on the ball, smiles and says, 'Sorry Melanie, I'm not marking you off.'

Everyone braces for impact. Suddenly it's lunchtime for everyone. Gary looks at me and shrugs. John's disappeared. Melanie looks different than she looked an hour or so ago. Pupils dilated, sweating; she most likely met her boyfriend in a less-frequented city carpark to take drugs. But when this fictional, yet potentially very real boyfriend realised she left the appointment (money for drugs) early, he forced her to come back and do whatever is necessary to be marked off as attended. Melanie could have a sympathetic ear if everyone wasn't so scared of losing their own jobs. They ignore her obvious distress. Rodney isn't budging. I take a gamble. 'Hey Melanie, you ok?'

Rodney snaps his head in my direction. Wendy, the receptionist, puts her headphones on. Melanie looks at me. I try to connect. 'Rodney has done this to me too, but he's not such a bad guy, are you Rodney?'

Melanie is sweating and afraid and it's obvious it's not an act. Rodney seems to be reconsidering his situation re Melanie when an office door opens across the room. A slim, tanned woman wearing a white pant suit and high heels, who looks like she's just stepped off a private jet, confronts Melanie. Apparently, this woman is the general manager, here to streamline the joint. She speaks aggressively in a thick accent, French, I think? Even if I wanted to intervene, this situation has become layered and treacherous, and I need my money too. I do what everyone else does: slink off to the side and do nothing as two security guards appear. They take Melanie away.

Out on the bustling street I see Melanie sitting on the footpath, the two security guards standing over her. She's smoking, taking big drags on her ciggy. No talk. Just smoke, and the city.

10
Yarraville *Rififi*
My Life in Cinema and Crime

Back when I was ten I started going to the Sun Theatre in Yarraville all the time. It was a big old art deco building that had fallen into disrepair in the previous decades, but around 1997, it was resurrected as a film society. It had an enormous 1000-seat auditorium, one screen, and barely anyone ever went. The film society only showed films on the weekends, mostly black and white stuff. Films like *Rififi*, Jules Dassin (1955) and *Asphalt Jungle*, John Huston (1950). I saw *Le Cercle Rouge*, Jean Pierre Melville (1970) and soaked it up like a cinematic sponge. Melville went all out with the set pieces. Whether it's a sleek mahogany interior of a train compartment clunking through the countryside or a lonely ornate diner straight out of an Edward Hopper painting, Alain Delon is there, stalking the landscapes of the film, the collar of his cream-coloured trench coat popped, hands in pockets, crystal-blue eyes staring into the camera. I remember seeing *The Driver*, Walter Hill (1978) with Ryan O'Neal as the cold, expressionless getaway driver for hire. Obsessive, strong, streetwise: these were virtues.

On the roof of the cinema was a neon sun that would buzz on at night. There were mauve seats with gold trim and the lobby was like stylish swirls of marble ice cream. The candy bar had very buttery popcorn. Every time you went to see a film, you'd get a circle on your membership card crossed off. I often had 999 seats to myself, and I sat smack bang in the centre. If anyone else came in the cinema to see a film, I took it personally, like someone had just walked into my house. From the age of ten onwards, I would go to see as many films at the Sun as possible. My parents would also take me to the Astor and the Kino, and to action films at Greater Union.

My dad was a heist film fan, big time. He liked gangsters and crime in general, but heist films with lots of planning-the-crime sequences were his bread and butter. I remember seeing *Rififi*. The meticulousness, the control and the authenticity of the crooks' world blasted into my head. The film dominated my celluloid-prone brain. After seeing the film, we came home and my dad went on and on about how deciding to show the centrepiece of the film all in silence was a masterstroke. I agreed. We didn't agree on much at the time, but if it was anything heist-related, we got along well. I got deep into those specific cinematic worlds and everything that came with it. I revelled in the thieves' lives I saw onscreen. The grimmer the better. They had strong codes of honour. They had gallows humour. They knew how to use violence. They were men with specialisations. I wanted to be like them. I wanted to know everything about thieves. I would go to the library and read up about heists on the internet, which had just become available, and borrow true crime books. I was excited to find out that Melbourne has a rich history of organised crews of professional armed robbers doing their thing. We've got Ray Bennett, also known as Ray Chuck, or The General, the mastermind of the infamous Great Bookie Robbery in 1976. An old-school crook in a class of his own. He was one of the greatest armed robbers in Australia. Also Russell 'Mad Dog' Cox, who was on the run for eleven years from 1977–1988. A prolific armed robber. A murderer. A vegetarian and an exercise nut. He was recaptured at Doncaster Shopping Centre car park, by detective Paul 'The Fish' Mullet. We've also got dibs on the notorious 'Road Gang Robbery' in Richmond in 1994, when thieves dressed up as a crew of road workers in high-vis stole $2.4 million from an Armaguard van and got away. I didn't read all that much throughout my teen years but all the reading I did was crime related. I printed off all the newspaper articles I could find on that particular heist. I sourced academic studies on the psychological profiles of professional thieves. I read government reports on increased security measures to stop bank robbery. Melbourne was the bank robbery capital in the 1980s. Shit was hectic back then. I read all about it.

Nearly everyone I hung with shoplifted. It was a normal thing to do. But my fixation for thieves would blossom into something else entirely. I was an intense kid, and I took my obsessions seriously. It wasn't long before I first got caught shoplifting. I was twelve years old. Sure, I'd taken little things here and there, lollies etc, but when I got caught stealing sports gear from Highpoint with my friend Dwayne McTaggart, it was a different story. Dwayne and I were inseparable back then. His chain-smoking mum Rachel always had a pack of Holiday 50s on the go and wore a brown bomber jacket with a big gold eagle on the back with her red perm and gold earrings. She spent all the money they didn't have on getting Dwayne kitted out in the newest sports gear. Meanwhile, my mum got everything from the op shop like a real povo. I always envied Dwayne. That day at Highpoint started well, as I'd managed to steal a pair of Nike shorts from Rebel Sport by just putting them on under my pants in the change room and waltzing out. The security tag was still attached, but for some reason, it didn't go off. But when I walked into Harris Scarfe with the shorts still on underneath my pants and the beepers went off, the security guard grabbed me. I denied everything. Dwayne didn't steal anything, but they grabbed him too. The security guard took me to a back room to wait for the police. The police found the shorts and cautioned me. My parents blamed Dwayne, and said our friendship was kaput. I said it was my choice. They didn't believe me. They even made me change schools. After we drove away from the Highpoint carpark, my parents in their yellow Datsun 200B and Dwayne's mum in their Commodore, I barely saw Dwayne again.

Our family, my mum and dad and older brother, moved into my great grandmother's house after she died. My folks got the house for very cheap. Gentrification wouldn't start for another five to ten years. When we moved there, and had been living there for some time, one of my dad's friends remarked (I remember it as I was reminded of it recently) that I was like a throwback to a different era. The way I took to the streets so naturally was like I belonged to another generation. I was a rough and tumble kid who loved being out and about. We moved out of Yarraville to Footscray when I was around 14/15. We were living in a single-front weatherboard house that backed on to the train line. I really loved trains. I loved public transport, trains especially, and as my parents intermittently didn't have a car, we spent lots of time on trains. If there was a film set on a train or a film with decent sequences on a train, I made sure I saw it. Train films were a close second to heist films. A train in slow motion, a character walking through train carriages, pretty much anything train-related gave me a buzz. I remember seeing *The Taking of Pelham 123*, with Walter Matthau and Robert Shaw, a really good train/heist film. Or Sean Connery fighting in close quarters with a villain in a train compartment in *From Russia With Love*, big tick! Jon Voight as an escaped inmate in *Runaway Train* who takes over a train and fully embraces chaos and death while thundering through the snow. It's a mediocre film, but as the centrepiece is a train, it's elevated above its station and into train film folklore.

* * *

I hated school, and by this age I was barely going. Instead, I'd catch trains all over Melbourne. I'd pack my bag like I was going to school, with books, lunch, then travel across Melbourne, sometimes even as far as Frankston, by myself or with a few mates. We loved trains and we loved stealing. We racked clothes all over town. We did graffiti too. We carried black markers in our jocks and we'd tag whole empty train carriages, floor to ceiling. The old Comeng trains with the yellow and green colours were still operational then. They had carpeted floors and our thick black ink soaked nicely into it. There was no one around on the trains during the day, just us kids. Then I'd come home at school time, like it had just been another tough day at school. It was 2001. I was fifteen.

By now, I stole the things I was interested in, specifically, cans of spray paint, porn mags from newsagents, and specific brands of clothes. I started carrying two sets of pliers, one small and one bigger, for cutting beepers off clothes in case there were different-sized beepers on them. Myer, David Jones, Nike, I went in hard. The crew I hung out with at the time all dressed the same, little street athletes, and it was always about who could be the freshest, i.e. who looked the best and who had the maddest style. This freshness had to be obtained through shoplifting clothes. Once you'd proved yourself through risky racking achievements, then you could brandish your gains and glow on the street with pride, inside and out. We stole the two brands that proved your worth, Nautica and Ralph Lauren. They were the more difficult to rack. My prize possession was a bright white Nautica fleece, with a navy-blue yacht sail, worth around $200. I cut the beepers off in a change room in David Jones, wore it underneath a big jacket so I looked like a little snowman, and ran out. I wore that fleece everywhere I could, until I accidentally burnt a tiny ciggy hole in it, which in my world rendered it unwearable. The Jisoe documentary wouldn't be coming out for another few years, but I racked from stores like he racked from stores. Outside of cinema, Jisoe and his crew of graffiti writers and thieves were role models for how to go about it. We knew them personally. Jisoe was a role model for me. He sat atop the Graff game on his St Albans pedestal.

One of the hardest stores to rack from was the official Ralph Lauren store on Collins Street. I scored a navy-blue, long-sleeved cashmere top with a gold insignia from there. It was extremely soft like a little lamb. Back then, everyone was wearing Von Dutch hats, Ecko Unlimited T-shirts and boot-cut jeans. I hated that shit. I used to wear a black Nike jacket that folded up into a bum bag. Navy-blue Nike trackies for casual comfort. Columbia ski jackets in pastel colours with big hoods that I could hide my little head in. White Calvin Klein boxer shorts and baggy red and white Tommy Hilfiger polo shirts. I combined a slick sport look with the occasional baggy piece cos baggy shit was still mega popular. I even stole a pair of white Nike tailwind trainers that I put on in Rebel Sport and ran out. There were beepers in the shoes and they went off. I copped a chase from an overweight seccy but escaped down the Graff alleyway that goes from Bourke to Little Collins. By the time I was sixteen, I'd gotten into stealing porn magazines. But that particular interest had been piqued by accident with the first hardcore porn magazine I found. It was behind my house in Footscray. I was walking along the top of the canyon where the graffiti-covered back fences of the houses dropped almost vertically down to the trains running below. There was about a metre of rocky shrubbery ground to clamber on. I spotted it in the shrub. Snails had eaten it but the pictures were still very clear. The babes in it were sleek and hardcore and it blew my little mind. I jacked off on the spot right there on the edge of the canyon, in a bit of shrub, as the trains clunked by below. I stashed it and went back there often. I took a plastic bag to keep the magazine weather- and snail-proof. One day it was gone, but that kind of porn stuck in my mind.

During my busy days out racking clothes and paint, I wanted to up the level of risk. I wanted to get more bang for my buck. And that came accidentally (how accidental is opportunism?). I wanted to get more porn. The mags I would get from newsagents were lame. I wanted European stuff. So I decided to try and get into the back of a porn shop on Elizabeth Street. I got in through an unlocked door and into a back room where all the porn was kept. I grabbed heaps of DVDS and mags. As I was leaving I opened some drawers and there was a yellow envelope that had cash in it. I grabbed that too and disappeared into the city. Unintentionally, I'd combined stealing porn with burglaries and was on an upward trajectory towards the top of the petty crime pile. At the same time as watching porn I satisfied my need for voyeurism of a different kind. Nicholas Winding Refn's output these days is an empty aesthetic exercise but back in the day, his *Pusher* trilogy was mind-blowingly good. Lots of aggressive movement. Scumbag behaviour. Lost-cause mentality. Tough and relentless.

At this time my parents were in a state of shock and disbelief at how things were going for me. My mum was doing occasional work as freelance journalist, but as the pay came sporadically, and my dad was employed for short stints doing whatever he could, there wasn't much money around, which was stressful for them. My brother was reasonably well behaved. My parents didn't understand why I was acting the way I did. They'd already been to three court appearances for shoplifting and criminal damage. Twice at Children's Court in the city and one other time at Sunshine Children's Court. These times I was cautioned, fined for the criminal damage, and warned about the path

I was heading down. I didn't tell my mum that I didn't give a shit and that as soon as I left the court, the experience meant nothing to me.

By 2003 I'd moved on to Magistrates Court. From little court to big court, but I was always in court for the pettiest shit. I was mad cos no one knew that I hadn't been caught for the more serious thieving I was doing. The reason I was here this time was for the stupidest thing yet. I'd been caught doing a tag on a wall in the city when I was drunk. Such an annoying pissant thing, but when the cops grabbed me (they were literally driving past when I was doing it) my tag was wet, but so was another tag near mine and I decided to say that it was me that wrote DOLPHINS ARE HUMANS TOO. I decided to say it was me so instead of getting in more shit for my tag, I'd say I was an environmentalist and I really did think that dolphins were humans too. The judge looked hard at me for some time, before he said, 'You think crime is a game son?'

I stood there in court with my father next to me. My dad was an upstanding citizen. But I reckon he liked being in court and around criminals. He seemed almost a little thrilled. He was decked out like he was going to some kind of event, maybe a gangster's christening. He was wearing black slacks, a white shirt, a baby-blue tie and cream trenchcoat. If this court scene was in black and white, he could be a character right out of *Rififi*. All he needed was a white fedora. I wasn't really listening to the judge. I was more interested in the other criminals who sat in the gallery behind me. I couldn't shake the feeling that none of this was real, though. The judge, the criminals, it was like we were all characters in a movie. My dad dressed up the way he was somehow amplified this. The judge continued, 'You're going to get one last chance to make new rules, otherwise where you're heading, you better learn how to fight.'

The last sentence caught my attention. I got into fights occasionally, but I didn't pursue fights for fun. I didn't like punching on. I wondered how long it would take me to learn how to fight. He continued, 'If I see you in my court again, you'll be convicted, and maybe even worse.'

He peered over his spectacles. I got my act together right there on the spot for the benefit of all concerned. 'Thank you, your honour, you won't be seeing me again.' I bowed. My dad said, 'Thanks your honour'. I was fined. If anything, I was embarrassed as I thought that all the criminals would think that I was just another petty idiot. In some ways I was. But I had various thieving situations on the go at the same time. I'd get caught for some stuff, like this dolphins bullshit, and not others. And it was the stuff I wasn't getting pinched for, the kinda stealing that the criminals in the gallery would be proud of, that I'd started doing in earnest.

I first heard of 'Searchin' as a specific type of theft when I met a couple of older thieves from Sydney through a bunch of dodgy older guys I knew. They had interstate warrants out for them and were lying low in Melbourne. I was out and about in the city. I told them what I did, how I went into back rooms of shops and stole money. And when I told them, they got excited like they'd met one of their brethren. They had a name for me. They called me a little Sydney Lad. A Searcha. That's what criminal kids in Sydney did, Searchin. Melbourne didn't have a word for it. In Melbourne it was just rackin and shoplifting, but in Sydney there was a distinctive criminal subculture and they called themselves Searchaz. Searchin was going after cash kept in back rooms of shops, opening tills when workers were distracted, daytime burglaries in office buildings to steal wallets or purses, pickpocketing. It was what I did. It relied on stealth, agility and speed. I liked being on the move, always prepared for action. My perspective had sharpened. I now homed in on aspects of my environment that I hadn't before. When I'd go into a shop, I'd look for the door that would take me to a back room. I would see where the exits were and whether the door to the back room had cameras on it or was visible from the counter. Searchin relied on moments of workers' lapsed concentration, distraction, quick movements. In and out. I narrowed my vision and it paid off.

I traversed Melbourne all day on the hunt for opportunities. I'd go to places I'd never heard of, rich suburbs out east like Auburn, on the Belgrave, Lilydale and Alamein train lines. In these suburbs there were lots of boutique shops for rich old people where they buy candles and cable sweaters. I also went down the other end of Melbourne, to Williamstown, also rich. I covered lots of ground. I got the perfect opportunity when I was walking past a florist at closing time off the main drag in Willy. The worker, who was alone in the shop, was taking the bins out. When he took the first wheelie bin out and around the corner, it took about 30 seconds. I counted. While he was gone, I ran in and hid behind some big plants at the back of the shop. I waited for him to come back for the second bin. He came back in, grabbed the bin and left. I had 30 seconds. I ran out from behind some plants, went to the till, hit the no-sale button, scooped out all the notes, fifties first, shoved it down the pants and got out of the store. I got the day's takings, about $900. That was a good day. Other days I'd get nothing. It was all luck of the draw.

By now, I was living out my fantasy world. I was committing an avalanche of petty theft. I was Searchin and doing burglaries. I was still going to the movies all the time. I saw *Sexy Beast*, Jonathan Glazer (2000). The stylised underwater heist where Ray Winstone wears the scuba gear with his cockney crew and gets the goods from the safety deposit boxes is a memorable scene. When *Collateral*, Michael Mann (2004) came out, it was the modern equivalent of the characters in the film noir I used to see back in the Sun Theatre. And through *Collateral* I found *Heat*. I'd come late to the game with *Heat*. I know everyone likes *Heat*, but I really really liked *Heat*. It appealed to me on a cosmic level. I got the DVD box set. Then I went through Michael Mann's back catalogue, and that's when I saw *Thief*, his first film. The opening scene lit up my nervous system. It's where James Caan breaks into a safe with an electro-magnetic drill, rugged and technically proficient and the scene cuts between his partner in the car with a police scanner in the alley and back to his up-close drilling technique. He's after diamonds and that's what he gets before driving off through the rain-drenched, neon-lit Chicago streets. That scene merged with an idea that had been lurking in my head for some time. I wanted to open a safe. In my short criminal career, I had yet to do what the old schoolers did, and that was to open a safe myself. Sure, I could thrive as an opportunist, but what about a planned heist where I opened the safe? Then I could be proud. I set my mind to the task but as a budding criminal autodidact I lacked criminal teaching. All I knew was I wouldn't use a drill. I'd seen the technique of opening a safe using a stethoscope in a film. That's what I would try. I had no one to tell me whether it worked or not.

My parents had a friend who lived in South Gippsland and we used to go and stay at their house sometimes. In the town, there was a bowling club. One time I was walking around the town, and I went into the club during the day to see if there was anything I could steal. There was nothing, no wallets, and the cash register was open and empty. But what caught my eye was a massive green safe in full view behind the counter. There were ads for Peter Jackson ciggies in shitty frames over the bar. A newspaper clipping of the 2004 premiers; Port Adelaide Football Club, plastered on the front of the safe. There was a groundskeeper around. But what I did do was find a set of keys on a board that opened the back door. I had to try three sets. So I had my way in. I figured this could be my big moment; this could be where I acquired a stethoscope and opened the safe like I'd just seen in some film (I can't remember which). But I had to get a stethoscope. I made an appointment with a doctor. It was a big clinic. I got there early. I walked around looking for the toilets and there were many GP rooms. I saw an empty room and ran in, saw the stethoscope on the desk and grabbed it. I coiled it up, put it down my pants and ran out. I had my equipment and now had to put my plan into action.

I decided that Sunday night would be a good time. I set my alarm for 3 am. I had a torch and some gardening gloves I took from the shed. I rode my bike down there. I put the annoyingly bulky gloves on and used the keys to get in. All was quiet inside. So here was my big moment, the moment where the thief uses tools and knowledge of equipment to get into a safe. My hands were shaking as I put the stethoscope up to the safe. The cold, still night made even the slightest noise sound like a bomb going off in my head. A car drove past outside. I stopped. I held my breath as though my breathing would give me away. I waited for the sound of the car to disappear. I went back to work. I turned the tumbler and listened: nothing. I turned and turned, but still nothing. No clicks. Where was the sound? Was I doing it wrong? I stayed there for ages, sitting on the floor with the stethoscope, trying to find the pulse of the safe. I kept trying to get the sound. But it didn't come. I gave up. It was the biggest anti-climax of all. I rode home and went to bed a failure.

That event had a strange ripple effect on me. It was 2005. I was 19 now. I thought about the judge telling me I had better learn how to fight, but I knew that I could learn anything if I needed to. But I remember not having the drive or desire to steal as much as I used to. I battled with this. I had always wanted to be a thief, ever since I was a kid. I'd come up through the petty ranks and at some point I would go to jail. I would learn new skills, and that would be it. But the life I had been living was getting boring. I wanted something new. I had a few grand stashed away that I'd saved up from rackin and Searchin and I decided to go overseas. I bought a return ticket to London. I'd play it by ear. When I arrived, I began working long hours in bars and on my days off I'd sleep in and go to the movies. Due to work obligations, I literally didn't have the time to steal. In light of this new non-stealing situation, I made a deal with myself. If the opportunity arose, I'd take it, but if it didn't, so be it.

I was wandering around Leicester Square on one of my days off when I found the Prince Charles cinema. It showed a lot of old films and had really good popcorn. It was usually empty, not just the cinema itself but the rest of the building was relatively empty too. *La Haine* was playing that day. I cruised on in and there were only two people sitting together at the front. I sat left of centre, right in the middle of the cinema. Even though I'd seen it three or four times it stands up strong. I love it. As the credits rolled and the couple left, I sat there in the yellow light and did my quick analysis of what the film meant to me now. It still meant plenty. On the way outside I noticed that the candy bar counter was empty. The register unmanned. I hadn't stolen any cash for almost six months, which was the longest gap in years. No one appeared. I ran behind the counter, swooped the till, got the cash, ran back round, and kept walking like I'd never broken stride. Out into the street, no worries, but at the same time I was weirdly overwhelmed by an emptiness that muddled the high. I walked across Leicester Square feeling odd. If the old buzz wasn't there and I didn't need the money, then why was I still doing it?

I came up with a plan. In my head I thought that if I stopped seeing crime films, heist films especially, maybe I'd lose the temptation? If I could go six months without a dip, then why not keep going? If I stuck to my plan, I would become a better person. And in some ways, it worked, purely as an accidental change in allocation of time. It meant I had time to do other things. I met less hectic people and became involved in social situations that would be described as nice. I toned things down. Yet I couldn't really shake the urge as I hadn't found a replacement for that unique adrenaline that seemed to only come from theft. I loved stealing way too much. I felt like a mish-mash of all three main characters in Wes Anderson's first film, *Bottle Rocket*. (In my opinion his best film.) My favourite character in *Bottle Rocket* is the Owen Wilson character, Dignan. There I am at the end of the film sitting in jail in a jumpsuit hanging out with my two buddies who've come to visit. We're eating burgers and drinking Coke and the landscape is very still. While we're chatting, a reality is solidifying. The reality that I've wasted a lot of time doing not much at all, specialising in neither here nor there. But as I thought more, maybe that was the best part, the hardest part, being comfortable in the neither here nor there. My high-level nothingness had allowed me to see both sides of the coin. I smiled as I turned off Leicester Square and starting walking through Soho. I put a hand in my jean pocket and found a 10p coin. I got a little joyous at my double discovery, inside and out, and was about to stop and flip it on the street like a little chimney sweep but I kept walking and gave it to a shit busker instead.

11
Testosterone

I was with my mum at a bus stop in Footscray when an old guy in a suede tasselled jacket stood next to me, and, as casually as you like, pressed down on my shoulders, while announcing to my startled mother, 'Not gonna be a big boy is he?' I ducked away. He wore a cowboy hat, and with his calm, clear blue eyes, he looked like one of those worn-down guys from old westerns. 'How tall are ya son?'

I didn't answer. I was nearly 15 years old, 5ft-3, but not that much shorter than some of the Vietnamese men who were walking past me at the bus stop. It was mid-morning on a Saturday. As well as Vietnamese men and women, there were silver-topped old Greeks doing their shopping on the way home from Footscray Market. Footscray in 1999–2000 was like 'spot the whitey'. Mum stood next to me, looked at the cowboy. 'Why is that any business of yours?'

His old blue eyes were in appraisal mode with the look that a footy coach has when he's singled someone out for a pep talk. He reached into a pocket of his suede jacket, pulled out a wallet, handed my mum a card. 'I represent the stables of Gai Waterhouse. Do you like horses, son?'

My mum took the card, passed it to me, looked legit. I looked at the cowboy. I told him, 'I'm fifteen and I hate horses'. He blinked, slowly. 'Well, that's a shame son, cos you're the perfect build for a jockey.'

My mum went to give him back his card. 'We're not interested, good luck.'

The cowboy nodded. 'No worries, you keep it. Just in case.'

Our bus came. We got on and shuffled to a window seat, shopping bags at our feet. Mum looked at me seriously. I'd been through three high schools already and would drop out altogether soon. She thought jockeying could keep me busy, and who knows, I might like it. 'Maybe you could be a jockey?'

I took the card from her, pocketed it, then ripped it up later.

* * *

After the incident at the bus stop, I now had to consider the fact that I was actually short, and not just little for my age. The bus-stop cowboy had looked into my future. His mythical presence on the street, the getup, how sure he was about me, instigated internal and external chaos and produced an intense paranoia. There was no respite from it at home, and it featured one of the most unlikely antagonists: Randy Newman. My parents listened to his music all the time and I enjoyed his mournful ballads about places I knew very little about. But then my understanding of irony was relatively limited, likewise my physical stature, and the track 'Short People' took on insidious proportions and felt like a direct attack.

I was developing a distinctly delusional worldview. And sought to validate the delusion that short man's syndrome was a real thing. I didn't even need to search far and wide to back up my theory (although I did), cos the evidence that being short was an unfortunate, shameful thing was validated by my dad, 6ft, whose favourite album was *Little Criminals*, favourite track, 'Short People'. The criticism began at street level, rattled through the music I liked and blurted out of the mouths of friends.

Instead of pubes, I got paranoia. I became extremely vigilant. On alert for any situation where I thought my lack of development might be an issue. Sometimes going full AWOL; other times I took risks of exposure. Exhaustive levels of observation. For instance, I became acutely aware of the sound and intensity at which piss hit a surface, equating the velocity of splash at either the bowl or the urinal with masculinity. Sometimes I poured water out of a bottle to add depth to my stream. I got my first proper girlfriend at age 16, but we didn't have sex. I don't think I even let her see me without a T-shirt on. And when I started stealing my mum's car, I had to sit on phonebooks so I could see over the steering wheel.

I can't remember how I heard about testosterone treatment, or from who, but when I did, I saw it as my salvation. A series of three injections in my bum over three months. Apparently, it would be as simple as that. When I suggested the idea of testosterone treatment to my parents, they were horrified. There was no way I would be allowed to have something so extreme; just be patient. But over a few weeks of nagging, guilt tripping and emotional blackmail, basically telling them it was their fault I was so short and that I'd been in hospital for so many different issues since I was small, why was my older brother so healthy, did they treat him differently, what was wrong with me, etc, I broke them down and got Mum to make an appointment with a specialist.

At the time, height had become a social issue; behavioural, problematic and medical interventions and solutions for non-issues were springing up everywhere.

* * *

The head of Adolescent Health in Parkville was Dr Susan Boyer, and that was who I'd come to see. Dr Boyer was 6ft tall with a fashionable haircut and I was scared at first, but her relaxed, intelligent approach put me at ease. Our first meeting must've been powerful cos twenty years later she appears in my mind in a snap, and her presence solidified further, when recently, Mum told me a story about how she'd been at a concert at around the time of my appointment, and how she couldn't see the stage properly as the person sitting in front of her was so tall, and that person turned out to be Dr Susan Boyer.

Mum, me and Doc Boyer sat in her big office and I told her how worried I was about being so small. She asked about how I felt about my body. I explained the crippling anxiety and extreme self-consciousness and all I wanted was to be physically like the other boys. She said she understood. Then I needed to be examined. Mum waited outside on my say-so. Doc Boyer told me to undress as she pulled the curtain round. I sat on the bed while the gentle giant checked my dick and balls in silence. Then she told me to pull up my pants.

Back at her desk, she made a couple of notes. Mum came back in and Doc Boyer, with her large horse eyes and gentle smile, told us that basically, I wasn't that far off from full puberty; I was just a bit slower than other boys. If I could wait a little while longer nature would just take its course. My mum agreed. Then, I told her I'd heard about testosterone treatment, and said that's all I wanted. Thinking back, I guess it was a bit strange that even though I was a pint-sized teenager I bossed all the adults around. At home. At school. On the street. Doc Boyer told me of a colleague of hers in the endocrinology department that could help. Mum went along with it, as she knew I would win at all costs. Doc Boyer informed me that given the seriousness of the treatment, I was to see her again in a week just to make sure. A week went by, and I basically kicked her door down. I was 16 by now.

Dr Margaret Fitzgerald was a leading paediatric endocrinologist at the Royal Children's Hospital. When she greeted me and my dad in the endocrinology department of the hospital, I was immediately suspicious. Was there a reason that the two women involved in helping me grow were exceptionally tall? It wasn't just Susan and Margaret's towering size; they both had an equine resemblance. Dr Fitzgerald had a strong chin, kept her hair pulled back in a tight ponytail, wore a pearl necklace, and was genuinely frightening. In my mind, it was like being attended to by refined horses. She stood eye to eye with my dad and asked if he wanted to come into the appointment. I interjected and said he was happy to wait outside, which I knew was true. My teenage years were awkward for my old man, not knowing how to handle things, maleness, it was complicated. He sat and I went into her office for our appointment.

Dr Fitzgerald's approach, the classic, cold procedural attitude to the most intimate personal scenarios, is the way the majority of upper-echelon specialists deal with patients in the hospital setting. It's a style I would come to know well over the years. Back then, I hadn't figured out that the only way to get through to someone of Dr Fitzgerald's ilk was to meet fire with fire. I sat opposite her and was told that given my circumstances it might be suitable for me to undergo a short burst of testosterone treatment. First, I needed to be examined so I went behind the curtain, took my pants and underwear off and waited. Dr Fitzgerald came in, grabbed a pair of surgical gloves from the cardboard box above the bed, got her large hands in them, moved my penis around like a joystick, lifted up my balls, let them go, and told me to get dressed. I swished back the curtain trying not feel like a little pork chop in a butcher shop. She was tapping away at her computer, and after a minute or so, she looked at me with her steady, hard gaze, and said it seemed as though I would most likely benefit from the treatment. I was given a follow-up appointment in a fortnight. She would administer the injections. Even though she terrified me I hadn't come this far to throw in the towel.

Dad came for the appointment and waited outside, like before. When Dr Fitzgerald appeared, she instructed me to go into a room where I'd have my first injection. I put on a gown, waited behind a curtain, and pulled my sleeve up my arm as that's where you have injections. But when she pulled back the curtain, she told me to roll down my sleeve and to take off my pants down instead. I was to have the injection in my bum. I looked at the oily white liquid in the chunky needle on the silver tray with the other paraphernalia, then up at her. And I did as I was told. She mentioned something about it being painful, but I'd had needles before – how painful could it be? The standard ingredients of one injectable dose of the testosterone are:

Testosterone cypionate: 100 mg
Benzyl benzoate: 0.1 mL
Benzyl alcohol (as preservative): 9.45 mg
Cottonseed oil: 736 mg

Cottonseed oil is used in deep fryers in fast food outlets, and to preserve the shelf life of mayonnaise, salad dressings or cookies. In the 1880s, it was used in oil lamps and to make candles, and these days it's used in insecticides, laundry detergents and cosmetics. The severity of the pain varies, depending on how much fatty tissue there is at the injection site. I had a bony arse then and I got a bony arse now. The needle breaking flesh was run of the mill, but as the oil oozed in, there was immediate resistance. Apparently, this was normal. So was the effect of its entry, which was a painful surprise, like whiplash. I didn't expect the pain to reverberate through my body the way it did, a thud jolting my whole body. I was immediately nauseous, and I almost threw up. As Dr Fitzgerald tidied the cubicle up, she tried at being human and said not to worry as the first injection is always the most painful, the body has to get used to it. I was embarrassed, like I'd been violated. She said I would have two more to complete the cycle.

I returned for two more injections over the course of six weeks with Dr Fitzgerald doing the honours. The pain was pretty much the same, brutal, the only difference was that I knew what to expect. They should provide mouthguards for the process. For whatever reason, I wanted to show this scary and elite horse lady with the pearl necklace that I could withstand the pain. After the final injection, I couldn't sit down for a day. I'd been fast-tracked from an extended childhood. Piggybacked my way to the front lines of deep teenage development, but when I landed on my feet, my world, and everything around me, was in fast motion. I had a whole lot of catching up to do. Half man, half clandestine testosterone lab kid.

At first, I didn't think that the all-consuming, sex-obsessed behaviour that took over my life immediately after the treatment was abnormal. The fact that I began getting erections so often that I literally had to strap my cock to my abdomen with my belt to keep it contained, was more of an inconvenience. I began stealing porn mags and wanking in toilets, multiple times a day. I started collecting $2 coins for peep shows, and I'd go into one of the dark booths in the city, drop my coins in, the screen would pop up, the stripper would do her thing. I always tried to cum as quickly as possible to save money. $2 got you 30 seconds I think, and there were times when I didn't need any more than that. My body had hijacked me. I surrendered to it. I didn't know anything different. What I did find troubling was why, soon after the treatment, I became obsessed with women fifty years older. But thinking about it, it probably had a lot to do with the fact that the two women involved in the excruciatingly intimate and embarrassing process of assessing my manhood, or lack thereof, their austere headmistress-like approaches, in the case of Dr Fitzgerald, her imposing physique and elite pearl necklace coldness, had a significant impact on my young developmental self.

Around the time of the injections, we moved from Footscray to an apartment in Balaclava. One night I was riding my bike home from a friend's house, through the park, and I saw half a dozen guys appear from the shrubs, then some of them paired off, disappeared. I slowed down to see what was going on. More guys appeared, then disappeared. I stopped my bike, and literally a second later, a middle-aged guy with a tan and no pants on, emerged from some shrubs right near me. I wasn't gay, but that didn't seem to stop me. I should've been scared or something. He walked right up to me with a condom in his hand and told me to fuck him. He had a grey hoodie, sandals, and a bare arse. He nodded to me, and I put my bike down, went back into the shrub and fucked him. It was over in few minutes. That's how easy it could be. The bare-arsed man was real-life pornography. Jacked up on testosterone I went to Alma Park as often as I could, solving my immediate needs. There was variety too. Old guys, young guys, fat guys, skinny guys. I tried everything. I had money to burn from all the stealing I was doing and I used up lots of it at brothels. I went to Ji Li's in Footscray where $120 got you a full service, Asian girls. Manhattan Terrace on Lygon Street and the grubby Far Eastern on Racecourse Road. I spent lots of cash. Sex cinemas too. If there was any pattern at all to my sexuality, it was based off how quickly I could get my dick in a hole. And the cohort that required the least dick work were gay men and prostitutes. My entrance to the world of sex, my reference point, was when I lost my virginity to a bare-arsed stranger in a park.

I turned 18. And when I looked in the mirror, I accepted what I saw. I was officially a human man. A year earlier, when it was my 17th birthday and the testosterone treatment had only just begun, I told my best friend at the time, and when he laughed in my face at the possibility of being 17, I was shocked and to cover it up, my knee-jerk response was that I was joking, and was turning 16, not 17. From that day on, I always pretended to be a year younger than I actually was. So, when my development caught up and aligned, I couldn't synchronise my internal clock, and my casual lie about my age to save face became full-time deceit. I even got a fake ID, like my friends all did, even though I didn't need it. I stopped celebrating real birthdays altogether.

When it was my real 19th birthday, I celebrated it as my 18th. If anything, it felt as though the testosterone treatment intensified the secrets. I now had multiple narratives to navigate; I was hypervigilant, presenting wildly different versions of self, with the feeling of extreme dislocation from any semblance of my true self; I was a conman who gained nothing from the con. Testosterone treatment is common these days. Although I doubt there'd be many 16-year-old boys getting injections, essentially, to be the 16-year-old boy they believed they needed to be.

I still hate horses. I remember a school camp at Ace Hi Ranch, where our cabins looked out over green pastures, but in the foreground, right out front, was where they kept the horses. Pepper was nice-looking, with grey, white and black spots like pepper, but she was an absolute dud and turned out to be the slowest horse of the bunch, stopping constantly and looking around like an idiot. One of the ranch workers who supervised the ride had to constantly pull his horse near mine to force her to move, and when he gave me instructions to move my horse along, it just kept zoning out, pissing, nibbling at any passing leaves. I had to stay strapped to Pepper for the whole two hours and by the end I wanted to punch it in the head.

After being humiliated by Pepper on the scenic ride at Ace Hi Ranch, we were on the way to breakfast the next day, and when we were walking past the enclosure one of the horses was getting an erection, but it wasn't just any old erection, it was a horse erection, and it was just getting started. We looked on in a grotesque amazement as it kept growing and growing and looked like it would never stop. When it finally stopped growing, it was like a throbbing stump, then as casually as you like, sprayed a gluey white stream of frightening liquid like a fire extinguisher till a pool of sperm surrounded its feet in the mud. Whenever I remember that I remember something else as well: two refined, long-faced, middle-aged women coolly handling my cock and balls as part of the process of making me a man.

12
City Fragments
Lockdown Diary 2020

April

Moved into a tiny studio apartment on the fifth floor near the Victoria Market. A week earlier, I broke up with my partner, and ten days prior, still high from an ice session the night before, I broke through the door of our empty flat with a small metal pole and a garden spade. My plan had been to come down from the high until I was ready to face her, but I'd lost my keys. The metal pole and the door were covered in my blood from chipping away. When I finally got in, all I did was panic further. I would have to explain this to her, so I said I rocked up to find the door in this condition and that it must have been some feral kids on the rampage, and cos there actually was a bunch of criminal kids living across the road in a flat, she believed it. I hid an iPad to make it look like a burglary. The police came, the police agreed, the police left. A week later I broke up with her and moved into the cube.

Mid-April
Young guy coming out of the lifts with no mask, casually as you like. Melbourne has 900 cases a day. I notice his limp. I don't care. No mask, with a potentially ornamental limp?

'Hey man, how come no mask?' I gesture as he walks past, my hand over my mouth, and shrug for emphasis.

He's young, long hair, slimy. He's taken aback.

'Are you a cop?'

'No I'm not, and who cares if I am or not. I live in this building.'

'It's none of your business!'

'Fucken oath it is!'

He gets flustered and for a second, I think he might have a brain injury. It's not a good look to accost a person with a genuine disability. But I power on, backing myself. He rummages aggressively in the pocket of his baggy jeans and pulls out a crumpled bit of paper.

'I've got a medical exemption! I've got asthma.'

I thought he was gonna say he's got some kind of serious medical condition, but asthma, I have bad asthma too. Unless you're dragging an oxygen tank around, having a lightweight mask is not gonna make it too hard to breathe. I tell him, 'I've got asthma too.'

He steps it up and pulls more crumpled paper from other pockets; I see letterheads and some text. He's waving them at me. He's well prepared, spiel and crumpled official-looking papers to back up his claim. He turns and walks away in a huff.

May

The whole city is suddenly under construction, and there's a mammoth project underway right outside. The workers act as though they own the joint, directing traffic with their signs, do this, do that. I wonder why everyone obeys them when they actually have no authority in the public sphere whatsoever. Outside, past my double-glazed glass sliding door the racket is ridiculous. To build what they need to build, they've built a tiny satellite town raised up off the street consisting of five or six boxes connected by a walkway from one side of the street to another. They're building a towering apartment block. Only thing moving in the city are the buildings which keep going up. Cold weather. The threat of a storm hanging low over the city.

June
I wake up when the thing that looks like an old-fashioned oil pump starts pecking into the concrete. Follow the routine. Clockwork in the cube. Breakfast on the balcony. Collage of every cold day that ever existed. I look directly below, and the construction workers have set up their miniatures. Miniature boom gate and a miniature traffic light system like that miniature traffic school in Balwyn, with all the big toys that the young drivers have to navigate. This morning I read a story about a man shooting at a jet ski from a houseboat.

Mid-June
I start looking up guns. In particular, handguns. A few days prior I paid for a VPN, which is 95 per cent for the movies I download, but also for the bursts of potentially monitorable behaviours, such as looking at handguns online. Surprised to see that I could buy a Beretta M9 22LR, nine-shot clip, in black, for $900. That seemed cheap. As I was looking at the details of the weapon, I couldn't help thinking that if I wasn't careful, I'd end up like Travis Bickle. But would that be so bad? Social justice, cowboy style. The gun shop was called the Gun Emporium and was out near Tullamarine airport. Gun sales were through the roof. Paranoid stockpiling. Toilet paper and guns. But this wasn't America. I asked a mate if he would drive out to the Gun Emporium with me. I called Pat.

'What? You gettin approved for a gun, haha!'

He wasn't anti the idea as a whole but was definitely anti me getting a gun.

'Why not?'

He paused.

'Red flags ya cunt, are you serious? Wouldn't you have heaps?'

I hadn't considered that.

Late June
The notorious City Edge Apartments on the corner of Elizabeth and A'Beckett streets, a block down from where I live, have made going out at night semi-dangerous. I walk down the hill from on to Elizabeth Street, past City Edge to do my shopping. Before the pandemic I used to go there to get drugs from a little guy with long hair who sometimes wore a black smock that made him look like a bat. He lived on the top floor and as soon as it got dark, he would turn on a system of intermingled $2 Asian gift shop lights that wrapped around his balcony handrail, through chair legs and pooled in his windowsills. A flashy little guy. Flickering and flashing pinks, greens and blues all night long. It meant he was on. In 2015, firefighters responding to a blaze in an apartment in City Edge uncovered a clandestine meth lab.

The purity of the ice differed dramatically from week to week during the pandemic. I remember vividly the change in purity and the rise in price, cos one night I was smoking quality cold and then a week later, it was less than half as good. I complained to the dealer about this. Asked how what he sold me only a week ago could be so different? He apologised and said it was like that everywhere. Locals took the initiative and cooked it themselves, but it was pretty average. Disruption of transport, shipping lanes, air traffic, the logistics required for smooth movement were compromised as entry to the country closed up.

July

Lawlessness everywhere in the city. There seem to be no cops around. And when cops do appear, it's in plainclothes coming out of apartment complexes holding big brown evidence bags. Ram raids increase. Collins Street gets hammered by them. Every week a new report of an SUV or 4WD that's backed into a high-end boutique on the hill of Collins Street and fleeced it of handbags and other items. Brazen holdups occur. A guy dressed in a wig and holding a syringe walks into a jeweller on Collins Street during the day, pulls a small hammer from his pants, shatters a glass container, steals a $100K watch and rides away on a pushbike. A middle-aged man stands out front of a jeweller in the early hours of the morning with a fishing rod. He casts his line through a gap in the shop's front window, hooks a necklace, drags it back through the gap and walks casually away like fishing for jewellery in the early hours of the morning is just another day at the office. But the necklace is a display and worth nothing. The CCTV is very clear. He is arrested at his home in Melton within 48 hours.

Late July

Early in 2020 I could go almost two months without using, but when the pandemic hit and I was in my glass box, I succumbed. Every two months became every month, which became fortnightly, then weekly. But in those gaps, I wrote. I was resolute about knuckling down and working on my craft. Life for me was centred around take-away food, alcohol, cigarettes, drugs, and haircuts. Get a meal, have a drink and a smoke, get high, get dishevelled and then get a haircut.

August (last week of lockdown)

At 3 am I hear the swerve, accelerate, brake. Out the front of a four-star hotel diagonally opposite me a teenage girl is being handcuffed and put into the back of a divvy van. In two minutes, there's three divvy vans, plainclothes cops, undercover cars, and all I can see is one raggedy teenager. The next day I found out she'd tried to rob the concierge, pulled a knife on him at the reception desk.

It's early evening and I'm lying in bed, looking out. The building was finished. The little village had gone. I looked up at the tenth floor of another building as movement caught my eye. I was sure I was looking at a bored office babe looking at me and masturbating. I started masturbating. But after a moment, she lifted a guitar up in the air to show me what the movement was. She'd been strumming a guitar that I couldn't see. I shut the blinds.

13
Running

It's 6 pm on Racecourse Road Flemington, and I'm fifteen minutes into the night run, kicking into high gear. The crisp autumn evening air hits that sweet spot in my throat like one of those ads for a lozenge and the blue night mixes with the orange glow from within as I get into my runners' rhythm. I break a sweat as I run over the Racecourse Road bridge, turn sharp right down the track to meet the Moonee Ponds creek trail. I feel powerful, clean.

It's been six months since I had a flat-out ice weekend with 72 hours of talking shit with other pipheads, taggin, watchin porn for 24 hours straight. Now I live in the inner west, which has become my running track. Down Macauley Road, past Cassette Cafe, converted warehouse tower block apartments, long circuits back to the flat I share with Ro my girlfriend, after multiple breakups and reconciliations in five years. Living together is new. Running is new. Three four five times a week, now, pounding the body. Two and a half ks, 5, 10 ks. Sometimes I stop for a smoothie to carb load, get a tram back if I go too far, but usually it's a circuit home.

Home is a little flat on the bottom floor, then above us, just moved in, is a young, small-business-owning couple who clang up and down their boutique fire-escape stairwell that runs past our kitchen window. Right behind us, but still part of the same block, is a two-storey brick box with another young couple, public servants; on the other side of us is our next-door neighbours' Subaru, with the Save the World stickers parked out front. A little world of its own.

Out here, in the dark, train interiors, pale green, fluorescent, exterior metal whoosh, rumble past next to the trail. I'm halfway through my 8 km as I approach Macaulay Train Station where a few people wait for the train, tired, a little shabby, an Indian student looking lonely. A bunch of PSOs patrol the platform wearing their multipocketed fluoro vests, thumbs hooked out, like they see the cops do. I jog down and rise out of the underpass where the young alky kid sleeps, 26 but bulldog face bloated and lined already, cardboard bed tucked away for later. The tip of the trainyard comes into view. Concrete pylons lift the freeway up just for me. The trains behind the fence are sleeping, missing out on my run.

I speed up as I tackle an incline and glance at the muddy section of pockmarked creek beach below, arc down, speed it up, eyes front dedicated, and suddenly the world breaks in two down my left side, a jolting spasm in my left calf; the pain is immediate. Sharp. I try to keep running, acting like nothing happened, I make eye contact with a fit-looking guy coming the other way, disguising the pain in a righteous grimace. Fifty metres on it all collapses suddenly, leg comes out beneath. I veer off the track, limp towards the train yard fence, grab hold of squares of yard fence, three fingers each and look at the big stinking grain silos not far off. Sour taste in my mouth. I spit hard through the fence.

Fuck, fuck, fuck. This is serious. This is not a cramp, I reckon. This is a tear. I can barely move. I do some stretches; it'll be fine soon. The pain increases. I test my left leg. At best, the movement is a glorified hobble. Two skinny lyrca ladies pass with a bounding kelpie. I hate them. I feel like shit. Nothing more but a long hobble home. The sweat I'd broken on the run is drying and I'm getting cold.

I'm trapped on a section of the Moonee Ponds trail. And even though I can see the overpass next to Macaulay Station where I'd take a detour home, off Macaulay Road not far off, I think about jumping in the creek, swimming into the murk like an eel. Bikes zoom by in the dark. Joggers jog. I yearn for a curve in the track, somewhere I can hide, but it's all straight. I hobble up the ramp exit to the road and give my leg one last stretch, just in case. This section of Macaulay Road is always busy. I make sure the people in the cars see me stretch, and that I'm actually hurt, and not pretending to be hurt. I hobble across the road and turn into Stubbs Street, one of the straightest stretches of road. It's a nothing part of inner Melbourne overpasses and warehouses and the M Pavilion, blackpainted boxing venue and wedding reception centre.

Ro will be laying out the wine, making dinner. I'll be ages. Fuck. I want to get into a fight, attack an object, kick a horse, yell at a righteous boomer, something. Anything. The long cold street gives me nothing. Alone, flanked by factories. Ah, but all isn't lost as I could save up my aggression, stockpile it on the hobble, then unleash it on the hipsters eating tacos and drinking Mexican beer in the freezing cold, wearing those beanies that look like rolled-up condoms, their greyhounds in jackets at their feet. Yes! That's what I'll do. I get a burst of life at the thought, keeping the grim flame warm. Just you wait prophylactic-headed idiots, just you wait. I prepared my glare, got ready to unleash, but, as I limped in front of it, there's nobody there yet. I keep hobbling. I turn in to Flemington Road, hug the wall, onwards on the hobble, past the high rises opposite. Full trams, heavy traffic hurtling to the city or the airport, underneath Citylink. I'll be home in 10 minutes.

Up the hill is the Quiet Man, on the corner of Rankins and Flemington roads, and there's people taking advantage of the weekly steak and wine special. And suddenly the world is moving faster. Actually, I am. I close my eyes cos I'm not sure if it's real. The sudden lack of pain. Not possible! I feel the part of my calf where the pain was. I can't believe it. I've been so preoccupied getting my hectic aggressive message across that I haven't noticed the pain has been subsiding, that I've walked off the injury, and it's not as bad as I thought. A low-key spasm. I cross to my side of the street, to head for home.

Or I could just keep going. Through the cool sweat I feel the edges of the key card in my pocket. I legit could keep going. To the train station. Away from here. Where would I go? I see a hot flame lit under a clean glass pipe, a rock of high-purity meth melting into a days-long bender with no responsibilities as the sun goes up and the sun goes down and nothing matters except following the next moment of being so unbelievably high that I feel so beautifully numb and before I realise what I'm doing, my legs are powering ahead by themselves, I'm running faster feeling good, onwards, blood pumping into my thighs, feet pounding down. I open my front door; I escape the pain. I'm home.

Acknowledgements

For my mother, father and brother who taught me the ways of seeing, reading and writing. I absorbed your wisdom and learnt how to keep going when the going got tough. You endured so much. I love you deeply.

To Jeff Freeman for filling in the gaps in my family history knowledge and breathing new life into old Yarraville.

To Christos Tsiolkas for his immensely generous spirit and incredible support. And to my publisher Terri-ann White for taking a risk when nobody else would. I'm endlessly grateful.

To the Berry Family for their generous Fellowship. And to the State Library Victoria, that has been there for me in one way or another, from childhood up to the present day. I couldn't have done it without you.

And to all the friends who put up with me reading aloud and talking nonsense when I was cooked, and told me to pull my head in when the kick-on was done. Special mention to Pat (Paddles) Dare, Old Tommy Ames, Aidan (fresh legs) Smythe, Boys from the RS, WLS crews, Tom (milk bar days) Skrop, Chris (Lil Chris) Bartley, Nick (Nikos) Georgiou, and to any others I forgot, much love.

I first met Guy Rundle in 2018, when I received my Berry Family Fellowship, as he had previously been a Fellow. At the time, I hadn't written a word of narrative non-fiction, but over the next four to five years he became a mentor and friend, dedicating huge swathes of time, helping me to avoid cliches and fashionable writerly traps. As I honed my craft, he kept me on course. Guy Rundle is an iconic writer. Nobody else writes the way he writes. I'm so lucky and so grateful to have been taught by the best. I can't thank you enough.

About Upswell

Upswell Publishing was established in 2021 by Terri-ann White as a not-for-profit press. A perceived gap in the market for distinctive literary works in fiction, poetry and narrative non-fiction was the motivation. In her years as a bookseller, writer and then publisher, Terri-ann has maintained a watch on literary books and the way they insinuate themselves into a cultural space and are then located within our literary and cultural inheritance. She is interested in making books to last: books with the potential to still be noticed, and noted, after decades and thus be ripe to influence new literary histories.

About this typeface

Book designer Becky Chilcott chose Foundry Origin not only as a strong, carefully considered, and dependable typeface, but also to honour her late friend and mentor, type designer Freda Sack, who oversaw the project. Designed by Freda's long-standing colleague, Stuart de Rozario, much like Upswell Publishing, Foundry Origin was created out of the desire to say something new.